The Tolpuddle Martyrs
Injustice within the law

Herbert Vere Evatt

With a new introduction by Geoffrey Robertson

SYDNEY UNIVERSITY PRESS

Published 2009 by SYDNEY UNIVERSITY PRESS
University of Sydney Library
www.sup.usyd.edu.au

© Evatt Foundation 2009
© Geoffrey Robertson 2009
© Sydney University Press 2009

Reproduction and Communication for other purposes
Except as permitted under the Act, no part of this edition may be reproduced,
stored in a retrieval system, or communicated in any form or by any means
without prior written permission. All requests for reproduction or communi-
cation should be made to Sydney University Press at the address below:
Sydney University Press, Fisher Library F03
University of Sydney NSW 2006 AUSTRALIA
Email: info@sup.usyd.edu.au

National Library of Australia Cataloguing-in-Publication entry
Author: Evatt, H. V. (Herbert Vere), 1894–1965.
Title: The Tolpuddle martyrs : injustice within the law / Herbert
         Vere Evatt.
Edition: Reprint ed.
ISBN: 9781920899493 (pbk.)
Notes: Includes index.
         Bibliography.
Subjects: Loveless, George, 1797–1874.
         Tolpuddle martyrs.
         Agricultural laborers--England--Dorset.
         Justice, Administration of.
Dewey Number:
         331.88130924

Cover image: *Tolpuddle village* by Rhys Williams (1894–1976), originally
published in *The Daily Telegraph* in 1955. The original is located in the State
Library of NSW.
Cover design by Court Williams, the University Publishing Service

To M.A.E.

First published in 1937 under the title *Injustice within the law: a study of the case of the Dorsetshire labourers*, by the Honourable Mr Justice Herbert Vere Evatt, M.A., LL.D. (Sydney), with a foreword by the Right Rev. Bishop Burgmann, M.A. Th. Soc. (N.S.W.). The first edition was published by the Law Book Co. of Australasia Ltd, 140 Phillip Street, Sydney, 425 Chancery Lane, Melbourne, and the Law Book Co. of Australasia Pty Ltd, 21 Adelaide Street, Brisbane. It was set up, printed and bound by Halstead Press Pty Limited, Nickson Street, Sydney.

This second edition is faithful to the first. The main changes are as follows: the list of important dates at the front of the first edition is Appendix 1; footnotes have been converted to endnotes, some one or two sentence paragraphs have been combined, quotations of less than three lines run-on and quotation marks on indents have been omitted.

Contents

Introduction

Herbert Vere Evatt was a chief architect of the world's most important institution. His genius is present in the UN Charter, and in that post-war human rights triptych – the Genocide and Geneva Conventions and the Universal Declaration of Human Rights. He was the progenitor of the European Court of Human Rights and the International Criminal Court, both of which he proposed at the Paris Peace Conference. His international renown led to his election as the third President of the General Assembly of the United Nations. Why did this intellectual giant concern himself with the sad story of six Dorsetshire labourers, convicted in 1834 of administering an unlawful oath and sentenced to transportation to Australia?

Evatt wrote this work in 1937 while he was a judge of the High Court of Australia. He had earned Sydney University's highest accolades: his doctoral thesis, on the subject of the Royal Prerogative, prophetically pointed the way by which "dominions" like Australia and even colonies could attain full sovereignty.[1] He speedily acquired a practice at the Bar representing trade unions and his conspicuous brilliance enabled a Labor government to appoint him to the High Court in 1930, at the astonishingly young age of thirty-six. By then, the case of the Dorsetshire labourers was already celebrated: Sidney and Beatrice Webb had canonised them in their *History of trade unionism* published in 1894, and the Trades Union Congress (TUC) had recently published *The Martyrs of Tolpuddle*. Left-wing lawyers like Walter Citrine and Stafford Cripps QC roundly declared that they had been wrongly convicted. This particular legend, of working men who were victims of a miscarriage of justice, was inspiring for the union movement in the 1930s and today it has acquired a mythic quality: in 2009 Tony Benn claimed that the campaign to free them "was the turning point from feudalism to capitalism and socialism" while folk hero and folk singer Billy Bragg "credits the martyrs with the birth of the trade union movement".[2] But "Doc" Evatt (as he was affectionately known by the Australian Labor Party, few of whose politicians had doctorates) realised that the case of the Dorsetshire labourers stood for something very different, and something very frightening. He wrote:

> The Dorsetshire case illustrates the fact that oppression and cruelty do not always fail. Indeed, they sometimes succeed beyond the hopes of the oppressors. Unless trade unionists throughout the world are always ready to sacrifice their personal interests, their safety, or even their lives for the amelioration of the lot of the poor, their elaborate organisation may perish overnight either in a holocaust of terror and force or in the slower process of legal repression.

Evatt's analysis makes the case more significant. This early example of a workingman's combination was utterly crushed, by use rather than by misuse of the law. The government achieved exactly what it wanted – the suppression of a nascent trade union movement – through the fear and terror engendered by the savage sentences, emphasised by the desperate campaign begging mercy for the men. It was not the beginning of the trade union movement, but its end. The Grand National Consolidated Union collapsed and there was no causal link to Chartism or to the later resurgence of unionism in the 1870s. Although the judge and jury were biased and the sentences were brutal, the men were nonetheless guilty as charged: Evatt found no violence in the Dorsetshire case "save the extreme and horrible violence of the law itself".

This revelation of injustice *within* the law came as a shock to Evatt: it moved him to write this book (an unusual exercise for a sitting High Court judge) and it inspired him to think about the necessity for incorporating into the law a set of basic guarantees of human rights which would make "injustice within the law" much less likely. Evatt was appalled that statutes designed for one purpose could be used by one class for violence against another, "through the slower process of legal repression". His immediate solution was to endorse the jury system, so long as it is truly representative ("a jury consisting of the labourers' real peers, not of their bitter opponents, would certainly have acquitted them"). However, such "sympathy verdicts" are unreliable, as has been shown by convictions in notorious "Irish miscarriage" cases (the Birmingham 6; the Guildford 4) by jurors riven with prejudice towards minorities or emotionally intimidated by the prosecution or the tabloid media. Evatt gave the solution to "injustice within the law" more thought. Two years later, when H.G. Wells published his Penguin special, *A New World order*, arguing for a universal declaration of human rights, Evatt saw how such a charter, introduced into domestic law, could provide the necessary inbuilt protection against the kind of cruelty that had been so evident in the case of the Tolpuddle Martyrs.

That cruelty comes through to us today, even in Evatt's precise and lawyerly account of the proceedings against these good, simple, hardworking men. He explains the direness of their straits, as they laboured for rich landowners for a few shillings a week in a stratified society which allocated rank and station at birth, and which allowed, even after the 1832 Reform Act, only about 5 per cent of the population to vote at elections. The hopes engendered by the recent repeal of the Combination Acts, which had at least made trade unionism legal in theory, imbued intelligent men like George Loveless, a Methodist lay-preacher, with the idea of setting up a "friendly society" which might seek through collective bargaining an increase in their meagre wages.

They feared victimisation – hence the rather pathetic ritual of kneeling with a copy of the Bible and swearing to keep the union secrets before the picture of a skeleton whilst hearing the sepulchral injunction to "remember thy end". The rules of their society were hardly revolutionary: "that no person should be admitted to their meetings when drunk; that no obscene songs or toasts should be allowed; that they should not countenance any violence or violation of the laws of the realm".

But 1834 was the year when the Grand National Consolidated Union was established in London, extending even to women workers such as the bonnet makers, and the Tolpuddle society belonged to it. William IV, a King who despised his lesser subjects, demanded "some checks to the progress of this evil" (i.e. trade unionism). And Home Secretary Lord Melbourne, a Whig (i.e. a liberal) who ruled in the interests of the upper class, boasted in private correspondence with the King of "the mortal blow which it [the sentence of transportation] strikes at the root of their whole proceedings" (i.e. of national trade unionism).

When a vicious Dorchester landowner and magistrate, George Frampton, wrote to Melbourne to complain about this little Tolpuddle society, the government decided to make it a scapegoat whose fate would destroy the union movement. The six men were arrested under the Illegal Oaths Act. The statute was passed in 1797 as a result of mutinies in the navy and intended to combat seditious conspiracies in the armed forces, but its words were wide enough to catch oaths taken by members of friendly societies (and Masonic and Orange Lodges, whose members were, of course, never threatened with prosecution). A lickspittle judge, Baron Williams, was despatched to Dorchester to ensure their conviction – a certainty before a jury of landowners in any event – and to pass an unconscionably brutal maximum sentence of seven years transportation in order to discourage other would-be friendly societies.

Evatt tells the story as undramatically and as fairly as possible. He is angry, as a lawyer, that such an important case has been omitted from the "State Trials" – law reports that purport to record all politically significant criminal proceedings in Britain. (The reason is that the state trial series was "a Whig compilation", and it is likely that the transcript of a trial that would show the vileness of a Whig government was deliberately omitted.[3]) So Evatt sets about constructing as accurate a record as sources allow, set against the social reality of a time when, as Harold Laski put it: "the forcible suppression of discontent was an integral part of Whig policy" – a policy which the Tories completely supported, although even conservative newspapers were revolted at the savagery of the sentence.

Evatt precisely outlines the course of the prosecution, with the magistrate/landowners improperly encouraged by Melbourne and the Attorney-General (and by clergymen of the Church of England, always supportive of the upper classes in this period). Melbourne himself selected the charge and arranged for their speedy trial: his brother-in-law became the foreman of the Grand Jury which indicted the men! They could – and should – have been prosecuted summarily (i.e. before magistrates, not a judge and jury) for their pathetic oath-taking, but this would carry a maximum sentence of three months and the government wanted them put away for much longer. So its law officers opted for the more serious charge, a felony carrying transportation for up to seven years. Evatt describes the imposition of the maximum sentence as "cruelly unjust and disproportionate" and demonstrates that it was a political decision, since a few months later members of a much more active trade union branch who swore a similar oath were merely discharged on a good behaviour bond. The Tolpuddle sentences were designed to destroy the trade union movement – so these men were "martyrs" to that cause in the true sense of that word.

George Loveless and his five comrades were transported 12,000 miles to "Botany Bay" (in fact to Port Jackson, the harbour of Sydney), shackled to the debauched and violent villains for whom transportation meant a reprieve from the death sentence. For two years they toiled as convicts, while a protest movement – fuelled by a reaction to the savagery of the sentences rather than sympathy for trade unionism – gathered apace in London. A quarter of a million people signed a pardon petition and tens of thousands turned out at street rallies demanding that the men be brought back home. Melbourne remained hostile, as did Pitt, his brief Tory replacement as Prime Minister, but the fact that the sentences had been effective in smashing the trade union movement allowed the next Melbourne government to be more generous. The six were pardoned, and they returned to a hero's welcome in London in 1837. But nothing had changed for the better: as Evatt emphasises, society remained as class ridden as ever, the Grand National Consolidated Union had collapsed, and the privileged few showed no interest in sharing political power or economic wealth with "those they contemptuously termed the lower orders".[4] Further proof of Evatt's thesis is provided by the men themselves, who were set up with land in Dorchester purchased from the proceeds of a tribute fund. They were ostracised by neighbours, and George Loveless saw no future for the working class in England. Five of the six set sail for Canada, where today they are buried in modest graves in an Ontario cemetery. Neither the British Labour Party nor the trade union movement which now hails them as martyrs has ever thought to bring them back for burial in Westminster Abbey, resting place of British heroes, although the TUC does hold an annual festival in their honour in Tolpuddle.

Evatt was writing in 1937, as war clouds gathered over Europe and as Japan's militant nationalism had begun to threaten Australia. Laws in Germany and Italy had already turned trade unions into instruments of the fascist state, and Evatt was prescient in his perception that workers' rights would "perish overnight ... in a holocaust of terror and force" unless they were defended by the sacrifice of lives. He recog-

nised that obedience to such laws – the Tolpuddle Martyrs had accepted their fate with resignation – was no example for this time, and that
movements protesting only for merciful sentences were not a satisfactory response. The true lesson of 1834, that tyranny will triumph
unless workers are prepared to stand and fight, was a lesson that he
drew for 1937. Evatt's thinking in this book soon inspired him to re-
sign from the court and win a seat for Labor in the federal parliament.
When Labor took office in 1941, he became both Attorney-General
and Minister for External (i.e. foreign) Affairs – posts he held for the
next eight years.

Evatt made his – and Australia's – first international mark in 1945
at the San Francisco Conference which founded the United Nations.
My friend Michael Foot, then a young journalist, still remembers his
sense of awe at this gravel-voiced Australian who emerged to dominate
it. Evatt became the *de facto* leader of the small- and medium-sized
nations who sought to build an institution that would assist their development as well as their security. He led the fight against the Soviets
in an attempt to limit the "great power" veto, and the fight against the
United States to secure a pledge of full employment in the Charter, a
document which benefited in many ways from his drafting sugges-
tions. At the end of the conference Ed Stettinius, the American
Secretary of State, publicly declared that "no-one had contributed
more to the conference than Mr Evatt" and the Peruvian delegation
even moved a resolution by small powers to "pay homage to their great
champion, Mr Evatt". In the words of the *New York Times*, the conference had seen the exercise of two kinds of political power, the first
packed with heavy national muscle and coercion and the other pur-
veyed by force of ideas, argument and intellectual effort – and the
paper hailed Herbert Vere Evatt as the epitome of the latter.[5]

Evatt's far-sighted vision for the enforcement of human rights was
on display the following year at the Paris Peace conference, when he
was the first to propose the establishment of a European Court of

Human Rights, which would have the power to admit individual complaints and make binding determinations for that war-ravaged continent. He argued that even democratic governments could not be trusted to protect the rights of individual citizens, as they could be ridden over roughshod by prejudiced majorities. Only a court could give legal remedies that would deter other states from abusing their powers. The European Court of Human Rights was established in 1951 in Strasbourg and is the most influential human rights court in the world today.

As a result of Evatt's pre-eminence in San Francisco and Paris, Australia was elected to the UN's first commission on human rights and presented that body with a statute for an international human rights court. To arguments from nervous delegations that such a court would impinge upon national sovereignty, Australia's delegation, instructed by cablegram from the Doc in Canberra, feistily replied that sovereignty was "an outmoded conception, a fetishist survival whose worship should be anathema in the face of economic and human inter-relationship of our one atomic world". Non-aligned countries were mightily impressed and the UK and US were forced to concede the strength of the argument, although of course the Soviets opposed it from the outset and the Cold War made it unsustainable. It was later reversed by Robert Menzies, whose government opposed international co-operation in respect of human rights for fear that it would come to target the White Australia policy and the treatment of Aborigines. But it is a remarkable fact – upon which Australians rarely remark – that Evatt and his delegates were first to beat the drum for policies that Amnesty International and other human rights organisations were to take up again the in 1990s, and which today are beginning to come to pass.

Evatt's argument was that the fifty-eight nations then making up the UN had a duty not only to agree on minimal universal values but to incorporate them into a convention that would bind all nations and have enforcement machinery based on an international court. The Australians were proposing a convention to be implemented by a domestic statute in every country, which would require that country to accept the decisions of an international human rights court. They lost this argument through the hypocrisy of countries unprepared for any independent body to hold them to their pledges, but it is ironic to think that Australia, a nation that would subsequently shrink from adopting Human Rights, first earned its international spurs by its stance – widely respected at the time – in favour of a binding charter and an international human rights court.

On Evatt's instructions, the Australian delegation played an important part in many debates over particular articles of the Universal Declaration. It called the bluff of the Soviet Union and its highly strung puppet states when they wanted to change the right to "independent and impartial" courts merely to "open" courts. (Stalin's rigged trials were always open, but were never independent or impartial.) It stood up for minorities: despite the reservation of the great powers (especially the US with its "Jim Crow" segregation laws, and the Soviets with their subjugated peoples). The Australian delegation explained that human rights were all about protecting minorities from oppression, including the oppression of the majority in a democracy.

Australia had a fifty-year history of flourishing trade unions and Evatt was appalled to find these two words unmentioned in the first draft of the Universal Declaration, so he insisted on inserting them in Article 23.4: "Everyone has the right to form and to join trade unions for the protection of his interests". Evatt's greatest achievement was to ensure the Universal Declaration included social and economic rights – for example, to minimum standards of health and housing. Mrs Roosevelt, who chaired the drafting committee, remarked that rights needed to be universal and not just "for a progressive state like Australia", but she accepted that economic and social rights should at least feature in the declaration. Hence Article 22:

Everyone, as a member of society, has the right to social security and is entitled to realisation, through national effort and international co-operation and in accordance with the organisation and resources of each state, of the economic, social and cultural rights indispensable for his dignity and the free development of his personality.

And so it was that the man who had been so concerned by the fate of the Tolpuddle Martyrs that he wrote this book about their case later came to ensure that the rights for which they had been sacrificed were written into the Universal Declaration, including:

Article 23: The right to work; to equal pay for equal work; to just remuneration; and the right to join trade unions

Article 24: The right to reasonable working hours and periodic holidays with pay

Article 25: The right to an adequate standard of living, including food, clothing, housing and medical care and benefits in the event of unemployment, sickness, disability, widowhood or old age.

Evatt's Presidency of the UN General Assembly was a tribute to his international standing. On 10 December 1948 he received the Universal Declaration from Eleanor Roosevelt, who described it as "the Magna Carta for mankind". The previous day he had unveiled the Genocide Convention, the brainchild of Raphael Lemkin, a Polish lawyer. Evatt had taken Lemkin under his wing as soon as he recognised (and he was one of the first to do so) the importance of forging an international criminal law that would require state intervention against any regime that embarked upon the mass murder of its own people for racial or religious reasons. This too was an historic moment, Evatt declared:

Today we are establishing international collective safeguards for the very existence of such human groups ... whoever will act in the name of the United Nations will do it on behalf of universal conscience as embodied in this great organisation. Intervention of the United Nations and other organs which will have to supervise application of the Convention will be made according to international law and not according to unilateral political considerations. In this field relating to the sacred right of existence of human groups we are proclaiming today the supremacy of international law once and forever.[6]

A few months later came the Geneva Conventions – requiring humane treatment of prisoners of war and laying down rules to protect civilians in war time. These three instruments now form the human rights triptych and Evatt – representing a nation of only seven million people – had played a crucial part in their design and in their acceptance as the basis for a new international human rights law. Sean McBride, the Irish Foreign Minister of the time, once told me that he regarded Evatt as the statesman who most contributed to this crucible period for modern history.

But prophets are not honoured in their own country. In today's Australia, Doc Evatt is perceived as a political failure: his leadership of the Labor Party between 1950 and 1958 was marked by bitter infighting and by repeated electoral defeats at the hands of the conservatives led by Robert Menzies. Evatt is, however, favourably recalled for his lonely, utterly courageous and ultimately successful battle, at the height of McCarthyism, against the Menzies' attempt to abolish the Communist Party. In 1951 the Doc put on his legal harness of wig and gown and had the Communist Party Dissolution Bill declared unconstitutional by the High Court. Then, when Menzies put the question to a national referendum, Evatt led the campaign which had the proposal narrowly defeated. But his mind began to crack and to falter as he reached his 60s. I will always remember the look of sadness in my Labor-supporting grandfather's eyes when, as a precocious ten-year-old, I taunted him about how much better Mr Menzies sounded on radio broadcasts than Doctor Evatt. "If only you had heard the Doc at the height of his powers". If only ... but I hear it now, unmistakeably on those old newsreels of the first UN meetings and read his name in books of UN history or international law. Ironically, there is seldom any reference to his political rival, Menzies. Only an occasional footnote about his failed Suez mission. Evatt, whom he so often taunted and outclassed on the national political stage, was the man who contributed so much more to the building of a better world.

It was as a law student that I was first impressed with the Doc, when I came across a judgment he delivered shortly after he wrote about the Tolpuddle Martyrs. *Chester v Waverley Municipal Council* concerned a mother who had suffered permanent mental damage on seeing the drowned body of her young son recovered from a roadwork trench, seven-feet deep, which the council had negligently failed to guard or to fence after it filled with rainwater and attracted local children.[7] The other judges cavalierly dismissed her claim for damages for nervous shock, despite the gross negligence of the council, because in their Anglo-centric male minds she should have shown a stiff upper lip: "death is not an infrequent event ... it is not the common experience of mankind that the spectacle even of the sudden and distressing death of a child produces any consequences of more than a temporary nature". (Decoded, this meant that the plaintiff was a working-class immigrant from Poland, who had to learn to be less emotional.) Evatt, in a passionate yet scholarly dissent, pointed out "the notorious fact that children of working people are frequently compelled to play on the streets" and that the council should have foreseen the trauma for parents of a missing child as they waited "in an agony of hope and fear with hope gradually decreasing". To assist his unfeeling and unimaginative brethren, he quoted from William Blake (*The lost child*) and from Tom Collins (*Such is life*) and proceeded to refashion the law of negligence to permit recovery in such circumstances. It was a masterly piece of jurisprudence, infused with humanity, which came in time to be recognised as correct in law as well as in morality. It was an example of Evatt's profound belief that humanitarian principles could be deployed by judges to develop a common law that would meet the needs and challenges of a changing world.

The world has benefited from his passion for human rights, in ways that his own country has overlooked. When Eleanor Roosevelt presented him with the Universal Declaration, he replied "millions of men, women and children, all over the world, will turn for help, guidance and inspiration to this document". They have – but not in Australia, where its promises have never been translated into law. This is despite the fact that the Universal Declaration was hailed by the General Assembly as "a common standard of achievement for all peoples and all nations", to be promoted by education and in particular by "progressive measures, national and international, for their universal and effective recognition and observance".

Australia, unlike all other progressive nations, has taken no national measures to secure the effective recognition of these universal rights by passing them into law – in other words, by legislating a bill of rights. The Rudd government brought a charter closer by holding a national consultation on the subject. The Brennan report, released in October 2009, demonstrates convincingly that the rights of the poor and vulnerable would be measurably improved by adopting a charter. That is the simple reason why the Doc, at his height of his powers, wanted Australia to adopt a Bill of Rights, and it remains the overwhelming reason why those who truly wish to benefit the working class should insist on its adoption as a means of preventing the kind of "injustice within the law" exemplified by the case of the Dorsetshire labourers.

Geoffrey Robertson Q.C.
Doughty Street Chambers
December 2009

Original foreword

The Martyrs of Tolpuddle speak across the years of the price by which alone justice can be set up on the earth. They accomplished little or nothing in their day, but they take an honourable place in the long story of man's struggle against the fear and greed of those who entrench themselves behind the privileges that property and class bestow upon the favoured minority.

Mr Justice Evatt has done a service not only to legal but to social history by telling the story again with clarity and careful documentation. It is not a pleasant story. The legal, political, and clerical professions combined to do a cruel injustice. The voices raised in protest were quite ineffectual at the time, which shows that public opinion was as yet insensitive to the fate of England's worst paid labourers.

It is no doubt true that the great artist can never adequately express himself. The material medium which he must employ is in a lower order of being and, therefore, forever incapable of expressing what he sees and hears. So also religion seeks to express itself in the historic churches. But churches are always inadequate and quickly become institutions interested in a theology that stabilises social conventions, institutions which are only occasionally disturbed by the spirit of religion. So also courts of law are the instruments by which the dominant opinion finds momentary legal expression. Justice struggles to get in a word and is more or less successful according to the depth and the kind of human passions which are stirred at the particular moment.

Neither churches nor courts rise much above the prevailing opinion of the time, and that is why the spirit of truth and justice must whisper in the ear of individuals who will listen and respond and suffer, if need be, till the consciences of the majority begin to awaken. These social and moral pioneers are the one ground of hope that man may yet become civilised.

E.H. Burgmann
Bishopthorpe,
Goulburn, N.S.W.

I

The importance of the case

The great case of the six Dorchester labourers, George Loveless, James Loveless (his brother), Thomas Standfield, John Standfield (his son), James Hammett and Joseph Brine, who in 1834 were sentenced to seven years transportation to Australia for administering unlawful oaths, is only partly rescued from the comparative obscurity to which legal historians had long consigned it. The case was omitted from an adequate report, even in the New Series of the State Trials, which were devised in 1875 to fill the gap left from the year 1820, at which Howell's reports ceased. The selection of these New Series reports was made by a large Committee, the editor being the late Sir John Macdonell. "The principle adopted," it was said, "was to publish such cases as appeared to be of the greatest historical importance or to raise new points of law".[1]

How, upon this principle, a full report of the trial of the six labourers came to be omitted, it is difficult to say. The only reference to it is in Vol. III, Appendix A, where thirteen lines are devoted to the subject (pp. 1280–81)! The name of the chief defendant is spelt Lovelass, repeating the error in Carrington and Payne's law reports, the correct name having been given in the other contemporary report – that of Moody and Robinson.[2] According to Sir Gerald Hurst,

> The legal importance of R.V. Loveless has ... long since sunk to insignificance. The Unlawful Oaths Act has never been repealed, but it is obsolete. On the other hand, the case fills a niche in Eng-

lish social and economic history. No trial throws more vivid light on the conditions which led to the growth of trade unions, and on the difficulties which their pioneers had to overcome.[3]

It may be added that the case is certainly of great importance from the point of view of legal history and the general principles of the administration of criminal law.

In 1934, the centenary of the conviction was responsible for arousing certain interest in the case, and the publication by the Trades Union Congress General Council of *The book of the Martyrs of Tolpuddle* was a notable achievement.[4] But that work necessarily lacks unity of treatment, representing, as it does, the views of many persons. A supplementary study of the case may not be without value.

II

Social and economic background

In 1830 the agricultural labourers of England were seething with discontent and late in the year there was considerable rioting.[1] The violence in Dorsetshire did not extend beyond the destruction of the threshing machines.[2] However, an irregular body of 200 horse and 2,000 foot was formed by the landowners.[3] It was the time of "Captain Swing", and the house of James Frampton, the wealthy Dorset magistrate, was actually put into a state of defence.[4] At the Special Commission in Dorset in 1831: "One man was transported for life and eleven for seven years; fifteen were sentenced to various terms of imprisonment; seven were acquitted".[5] It is unlikely that the troubles of 1830 were forgotten in the affair of 1834 when Frampton again played a prominent part.

Labourers' low standard of living

In the late summer of 1833, agricultural labourers in England had an average wage of 9s 4d per week. It was then that the labourers of Dorset "heard from their employers that their weekly wages, which had been 9/- and 8/- but were then 7/- were to be reduced to 6/- per week".[6]

In an important speech in the Commons on June 25, 1835, Dr Wakley pointed out that although a number of trade unions were active in London from July 1833, the Agricultural Union was not formed at Tolpuddle until four months later, in November. As many hundreds of workers had joined the urban unions, the authorities might fairly be regarded as having condoned any illegality in union organisation which usually included an elaborate ritual and oaths of secrecy and of loyalty to the union. When the Dorsetshire labourers received notice that their wages were to be reduced from 7/- to the starvation wage of 6/- a week, they were (according to Wakley) practically compelled to communicate with organisers of other unions with a view to improving their own conditions.

Formation of union at Tolpuddle

Firth and Hopkinson state that two delegates from the Grand National Consolidated Union visited Tolpuddle in October 1833 and explained how the organisation of an Agricultural Workers' Union should be commenced.[7] At any rate, in November, the two brothers Loveless formed a union called the Friendly Society of Agricultural Labourers. It is also stated by Firth and Hopkinson that the union was formed on December 9, 1833, under the name of the Grand Lodge of Tolpuddle of the Agricultural Labourers Friendly Society.[8] These authors mistakenly refer the inauguration of the union to the day on which Legg, who subsequently became an informer, was admitted thereto. The union was formed at some earlier date, probably in November.

Ceremony of initiation

Hurst describes the procedure of initiation into the union, mentioning the evidence of Lark and Legg, the two informers called at the trial. As he says: "Arts which now seem supremely ingenuous were practised in order to give the Union a hold on simple men's imaginations".[9] The life size sketch of a skeleton was part of the apparatus, the Bible was kissed, and the entrant was admonished to remember his end. This spectacular ritual did not (in Dorset) in any way imply any threat of violence, but was only intended to secure loyalty and secrecy.[10]

Real objection was to trade unionism

The book published in 1934 by the General Council of the Trades Union Congress describes itself as the story of the Dorsetshire labourers "who were convicted and sentenced for forming a trade union". In point of legal form, the men were convicted, not for forming a trade union, but for administering unlawful oaths of secrecy to members and entrants.[11] The real objection of the Government was to trade unionism as such, as will be apparent from the recently disclosed correspondence which I analyse later.

Union organisation in 1833

Mr G.D.H. Cole has pointed out that "in 1824 the repeal of the Combination Acts had for the first time set the workers free to organise openly on Trade Union lines".[12] But it was not until 1832 that the trade union movement began and it was Robert Owen's leadership which caused its rapid growth in 1833 and 1834. Cole says that:

> By the middle of 1833, Owen had become established as the recognised leader of the Trade Union movement. The great stirring of the workers seized hold of his lively imagination, always ready to embrace millennial possibilities. The new era was dawning; within six months or a year the old system with all its evils, would have passed away, and the new age of co-operation would have begun.[13]

In their turn, the employers sought to prevent the employment of unionists. There were three great strikes in November 1833, and further strikes and lockouts early in 1834.[14] Owen's Grand National Consolidated Union greatly increased in apparent strength during this period, its membership in March 1834 exceeding 500,000.[15] This growth struck fear into the hearts of Whigs and Tories alike.

III

The politicians and trade unionism

Hurst's explanation of the Dorchester case is that the dominant political theory of 1834 was that combinations among the working classes "must have the effect of diminishing capital and, consequently, the means of employing labour".[1] It was argued that violence could not be dissociated from trade union activities and organisation.

Attitude of the Whigs

On his return to England after transportation George Loveless said:

> The Tories had their jubilee in the transportation of the Scotch martyrs, Muir, Palmer, etc.; but their atrocity was uncondemned by the mass of the people ... The Whigs have had *their* jubilee in transporting the Dorsetshire Labourers, Loveless, Standfield, and Co., *but their outrage was loudly condemned by all excepting their own* parasites and yet they persevered.[2]

In his article "A Travesty of Justice", Sir Stafford Cripps, K.C. takes the view that in times of necessity, to preserve the social order,

> the Courts, feeling the impact of this necessity, will almost always be ready to strain the interpretation of statutes and to bias justice in favour of the dominant class and against any whom they believe, rightly or wrongly, to be disposed to changes which may have the effect of upsetting the existing order.[3]

In his article, "Actors in the drama", Professor Harold Laski, after a careful analysis of the characters concerned, concludes:

The Whig Government was gravely disturbed by economic discontent; the recent Revolution in France had been viewed with great alarm by the governing classes; and the memory of how near England had been in 1831–3 to revolution was by no means forgotten. The forcible suppression of discontent was an integral part of Whig policy; the government had no sympathy at all with working class grievances. Williams' charge is inexplicable except upon the assumption that he shared these views and was determined to use his judicial position to attack their expression in a vigorous way.[4]

The Tories

Despite the arguments of Firth and Hopkinson to the contrary, the Tories of the time, though not directly responsible for the prosecution, were sympathetic with the Whig Government in the attack upon organised trade unionism. On September 26, 1831, Melbourne stated that, upon the accession to office of the Whigs in November 1830, Sir Robert Peel, the Tory leader, had pointed out to him that the Trade Unions were "the most formidable difficulty with which we had to contend".[5] This is corroborated by the fact that Peel, on ceasing to be Home Secretary, left a note commending "the whole of this correspondence re the Union to the immediate and serious attention of my successor at the Home Department".[6] Mr Henderson rightly said:

> The case of the Tolpuddle men never became a party question in the ordinary sense of the phrase. The Tory party in opposition never took it up even as a rod for the Government's back. Sir Robert Peel, the leader of the Tory opposition in the House of Commons, was as much dismayed by the growth of Trade Unionism and the disturbed condition of the country as was Melbourne.[7]

The letter of March 29, 1834 to Melbourne from Frampton, the Dorset magistrate, provides a clue to the inner meaning of the case. In this letter Frampton said that the greatest satisfaction had been obtained by the "higher classes" as a result of the sentence of transportation. The truth was, as Cole says, that "the rise of the Consolidated Union had set the governing classes and the manufacturers in a panic, and the Whigs were all for strong measures".[8]

But the Tories assisted so far as an official opposition could do so. The *Law Magazine* was definitely Tory in its outlook, but it strongly supported the conviction and sentence of the Dorsetshire labourers. This itself is striking evidence of the temporary alliance, for the occasion only, of Whig and Tory. For the *Law Magazine* contained so many bitter attacks on the Whigs that its restraint upon this one occasion is significant. Further, when Peel became Prime Minister after the dismissal of the Whig Government at the end of 1834, he took no steps to remit any portion of the sentence.

IV

Organisation of the prosecution

By one of the strangest and most terrible ironies, George Loveless, in his pamphlet dealing with the case, whilst condemning the Whig Government for their action, says:

> *Nothing particular occurred* from this time (December 9th, 1833) to the 21st of February, 1834, when placards were posted ... This was the first time that I heard of any law being in existence to forbid such societies.[1]

But, as we know now, the correspondence which commenced on January 30, 1834 and concluded shortly after the trial of the six labourers on March 17 and 19, proves that the local magistrates under the lead of Frampton were engaged with the Home Secretary, Lord Melbourne, in a daring combination to injure the Dorchester labourers, with the object of destroying trade unionism. The evidence now available is of the greatest importance, and careful analysis is demanded.

"Trusty persons" employed by magistrates

On January 30, 1834, James Frampton, J.P. wrote to Viscount Melbourne at the Home Office stating that societies were forming in the district amongst the agricultural labourers "in which the labourers are induced to enter into combinations of a dangerous and alarming kind to which they are bound by oaths administered clandestinely".[2] This letter also stated that the justices had decided to communicate "with Trusty persons in the neighbourhood and by their means endeavour to trace the proceedings and identify the parties".[3] It was considered that, even then, "they would still be under a difficulty in determining how to proceed so as to bring these parties concerned under the cognisance of the law".[4] Accordingly the advice and co-operation of Melbourne was requested.

Melbourne suggests prosecution for secret oaths

On January 31 Melbourne replied to Frampton stating that the Justices "have acted wisely in employing trusty persons". Melbourne referred the Justices to sec. 25 of the Act 57 George III C. 19, and also to the "Statutable provisions relative to the administration of Secret Oaths". [5] Sec. 25 of the Act 57 George III (passed in 1817) provided, inter alia, that all Societies or Clubs the members of which were required or permitted to take or assent to any test or declaration not required or authorised by law, or to take any oath not required or authorised by law – should be deemed unlawful combinations within the meaning of 39 George III C. 79. The relation of this latter Act to the Unlawful Oaths Act, 37 George III C. 123, I discuss later.

The true motive behind this suggestion of Melbourne is fully brought out in the brilliant interlude *The Dorsetshire labourers,* by R.S. Lambert, broadcast by the B.B.C. in April 1934. There Mr Lambert puts the following words into Melbourne's mouth at a scene in the Home Office in London:

> My dear Digby there is nothing I should like better than to be able to oblige you. But what you tell me about your village of Tol – what is it? – Tolpuddle, is nothing new. Here at the Home Office I have been pestered nearly to death with complaints about the growth of these 'dangerous and alarming combinations'. They spring up like mushrooms overnight in every county. Why, half of the Lord Lieutenants of England have written to me saying 'Can't Lord Melbourne tell us what to do with these agitators and their unions?' Here have I had a special report prepared for the Cabinet

by the Professor of Political Economy at Oxford himself – you see, we are nothing if not up-to-date, my dear Digby – and now his report turns out to be so fierce I daren't even show it to the Prime Minister. Stop the Unions altogether, says the Professor. Repeal the Act of 1825, and prosecute the leaders for unlawful combination. Well, we might have done that kind of thing three years ago, not now, since the Reform – well, I hardly think … I tell you what Digby, you tell your friend Frampton that the best thing he can do with his Dorset rebels is to look up that old Act of 1797 about the administration of Secret Oaths – the Act passed at the time of the Naval Mutiny, you know. It has been tried once or twice lately with advantage. They all have them, they all swear to secrecy, you know.[6]

Reshuffle of Law Officers

On February 22, 1834, Sir John Campbell was appointed Attorney-General in the place of Sir William Horne, and, on the same day, Sir Charles Pepys (afterward Lord Cottenham) was appointed Solicitor-General in the place of Campbell. Horne was to have been made a Baron of the Exchequer in place of Sir John Bailey, and Campbell was eager and anxious to be appointed Attorney-General.[7] In the end, Horne lost the position of Attorney-General and failed to get the judgeship. He had a dispute with Brougham as to whether he should be exempt from criminal work when appointed a Judge, and, in the event, it was Gurney who was made the new Exchequer Baron.[8] *The Martyrs of Tolpuddle* is inaccurate in stating that Horne and Campbell were Attorney-General and Solicitor-General respectively "at the time of the arrest".[9]

The magistrates' "Caution"

On February 22, a Notice or "Caution" was published in the district of Tolpuddle. It was signed by nine magistrates (including James Frampton) and four clergymen of the Church of England.[10] It stated that many labourers had been induced "to enter into illegal Societies and Unions, to which they bind themselves by unlawful oaths, administered secretly by Persons concealed, who artfully deceive the ignorant and unwary".[11] The caution went on to declare that persons concerned in such societies would be guilty of felony and liable to be transported for seven years. But no opportunity was given to the labourers to give up their union or to omit the oath of secrecy from their proceedings, for on February 24, only two days after the Notice, the six labourers were arrested and detained in gaol. On February 28, John Williams was appointed to the Bench. On March 1, E.B. Portman J.P., a neighbouring landowner, wrote a letter to Frampton in which he said: "I hope you have a complete case for conviction as that will crush the Union".[12]

Frampton obtaining evidence

On March 1, Frampton wrote to Melbourne stating that:

> I have at last obtained sufficient information on oath against some of the persons, who appear to be the leaders of this Society in one of the Parishes, to enable me to commit six of them for trial at the next assizes for administering unlawful oaths. I hope this may put some check to the proceedings; but I am sorry to say the nightly meetings are carried on much more openly than they were at first.[13]

This letter of Frampton suggested that the Government should either issue a proclamation against such Societies or offer rewards for the discovery of the offenders.[14] The letter emphasised:

> Our earnest desire for the welfare of these labourers, whose manners have undergone a considerable change and who are becoming very remarkably restless and unsettled since these Unions have been established.[15]

By this time, therefore, Frampton had succeeded in persuading or coercing certain labourers to act as informers. It is also reasonably clear that the real fear of the landowners was the combination of the labourers in order to secure improved conditions, and that the morality of secret oaths did not interest them. Further, Frampton was prosecutor and preliminary Judge at the same time, his object being, as Portman frankly put, to "crush the Union". As J.L. and Barbara Hammond said, in reference to the legal proceedings after the agricultural riots of 1830,

> It was inconsistent with the impartiality required from Magistrates who committed prisoners, that they should go on to mix themselves up with the management of the prosecution; in many cases these magistrates served again as Grand Jurors in the proceedings against the prisoners.[16]

Frampton's activities

On March 3, Frampton replied to Portman's letter of March 1, expressing regret that union activities were extending into Portman's portion of the County which he had supposed "had not as yet been infected".[17] On the same day, March 3, Melbourne wrote to Frampton acknowledging the latter's communication of March 1. He asked for full information and a copy of the depositions upon which Frampton found himself "able to commit six men for Trial at the next Assizes for administering unlawful oaths".[18] Melbourne doubted the prudence of a public proclamation or of an offer of a reward: "As such an Act would give Publicity to a State of things in Dorsetshire, which, as far as we are aware, has not yet spread in any other County".[19]

Frampton complains of statutory right of combination

On March 5, Frampton wrote to Melbourne transmitting the depositions and other particulars including a copy of the rules of the

Tolpuddle Society. This letter also transmitted a copy of a union leaflet sent to Frampton by the intermeddling Portman. The leaflet advocated united action and a strike for an advance of wages. Frampton also complained of the Statute of 1825 (6 George IV C. 129), secs 4–5 of which, although less generous to workmen than the Statute of 1824, did confer "indirectly upon workmen and masters a limited right to meet together and come to agreements for settling the rate of wages, and the terms which the persons present at the meeting will accept or give".[20] Frampton's letter also mentioned the caution published by the magistrates, and added,

> but the Labourers are taught to consider this paper as a mere invention of the Justices and not to be worthy of attention – an explanation therefore of the Law on this subject from higher authority than ours I cannot but consider as very essential and likely to be attended with great effect.[21]

On March 6 Melbourne wrote to Frampton stating:

> Lord Melbourne cannot entertain any doubt that you have acted properly in committing for trial these individuals, who are affected by the evidence you have transmitted; and the depositions, from the similarity of the Oaths and ceremonies which they describe, afford sufficient proof, that these proceedings in your County are a part of the general system, which is now attempted to be established in many other parts of the Kingdom; and that they proceed from some general directing authority. These circumstances will of course engage the most serious attention of His Majesty's servants; and the Magistrates of Dorchester will render most material assistance in this respect, by using all their efforts to obtain further information of the meetings which are taking place, and also of the names, description and character of the Strangers who appear to be traversing that County in the capacity of Delegates.[22]

Melbourne's letter of March 6 added that, although 6 George IV C. 129 – the Statute of 1825 – had "made a considerable alteration in the law", still "the Statutes upon which the caution, so properly issued by the Magistrates of Dorchester, is founded, are not in any degree impaired or affected by the provisions" of 6 George IV, C. 129.[23] The letter concluded:

> Viscount Melbourne would suggest to the Magistrates – whether it would not be advisable, that the prosecution should be at the approaching Assizes for the sake of promptitude in bringing the offenders to Justice – for the greater publicity of the proceedings, and for the most authoritative exposition of the law.[24]

Here we find Melbourne (1) selecting the charge which was to be preferred and (2) stressing the advantages of a speedy trial.

V

"The course of justice"

On March 7 Portman wrote to Frampton as follows:

> I hope you have a sure case for conviction as that will be very important. I find in many Parishes that the Labourers requested to sign the Church Petitions have declined doing so until they are assured 'that such signature was not against the Unions as they would not be bound not to join them'. Do you mean to proceed at the next Assizes? Ponsonby has written to me to know this fact as he will in that event do his best to attend. *It seems to be desirable to expedite the blow and to allow it to come from the Judges if possible at once.*[1]

The Ponsonby referred to in this letter duly arrived on the scene and became the foreman of the Grand Jury. He was the brother-in-law of Melbourne himself. Portman also appreciated the necessity for a knock-out blow, to be delivered quickly, and to be "allowed to come from the Judges".

Preparing for the trial

On March 8, Frampton wrote to Melbourne reporting that the labourers were declining to sign the Church Petitions until they were assured it did not bind them not to join the union. Frampton said that this appeared to him very serious as it showed the extent of the mischief prevailing.[2] On March 10 Melbourne replied to Frampton acknowledging the latter's letter of the 8th, and approving of the action taken in committing the accused for trial and in taking "precautionary measures to ensure the safety and the appearance of the Witnesses".[3] On the same day (March 10) Melbourne communicated with the Law Officers of the Crown (Campbell and Pepys). Upon Campbell's having accepted the office of Attorney-General, he was compelled to contest his seat at Dudley, where he met with defeat. He remained out of the House of Commons until later in the year, when he was returned at a by-election for Edinburgh.

Law Officers consulted

In the memorandum of March 10 from Melbourne to the Law Officers it was stated that various societies called inter alia "Trades Union" were corresponding with each other with a view to the "Increase of wages of labourers" and the "regulation of the time for working" and "establishing one common fund" for strike purposes. It was stated that at the meetings of these societies "secret oaths not to divulge or make known the proceedings" were administered. The Law Officers were asked to advise:

> 1st – Whether the Societies above described (independently of the administering of secret oaths) are within the 25th section of 57 Geo. III, c. 19, and whether the members of such Societies are punishable under the provisions of that Act or the Act referred to therein. 2nd – Whether the Societies above described in which are administered secret and illegal oaths are illegal, and how the Societies or the members thereof may be proceeded against. P.S. Viscount Melbourne is desirous of obtaining the Law Officers' opinion as soon as possible.[4]

The answer of the Law Officers has not been published. By Sec. 25 of 57 George III it was also provided that every Society or Club which employed delegates to communicate with any other Society or Club, in short, every "Corresponding" society, was deemed an unlawful combination within 39 George III, C. 79. The first question asked involved a consideration of Sec. 4 of the Act of 1825, which exempted from punishment those persons who met together for the sole purpose of fixing wages to be asked for by "the persons present at such meeting or any of them". It would appear that the Act of 1825 did not extend its exemption to delegates from different trade unions if they were otherwise liable to punishment. The second question is discussed later.

Sir Walter Citrine comments upon the fact that the six labourers had been lying in gaol for six weeks, yet Melbourne was deliberating with his Law Officers as to whether and how they could be lawfully punished. Citrine adds that:

> The reply of the Law officers is not on record, but it is evident that they did not agree with the Home Secretary. Lord John Russell stated on June 25, 1835, that the Law Officers had advised him to use another Act, viz., the Mutiny Act of 1797. Incidentally if it required the ingenuity of the most eminent lawyers to show the Home Secretary in what manner even a technical illegality could be proved, how could six humble agricultural workers have been expected to know the law?[5]

This comment is based upon the assumption that Melbourne's query was concerned solely with the Dorchester labourers. But it is probable that he wanted a general opinion as to the best means of suppressing *all* trade unions under the existing law. Citrine seems to err in supposing that Melbourne did not have the Act of 1797 in mind, for the letter of March 10 expressly referred the Law Officers to "The Statutes relating to illegal oaths".

Judge's reasons for maximum sentence

On March 17, 1834, the trial commenced, and on Wednesday, March 19, all the accused were sentenced to seven years transportation. In sentencing the prisoners, Williams said:

The object of all legal punishment is not altogether with the view of operating on the offenders themselves, it is also for the sake of offering an example and warning, and accordingly, the offence of which you have been convicted, after evidence that was perfectly satisfactory, the crime, to a conviction of which that evidence has led, is of that description that the security of the country and the maintenance of the laws on the upholding of which the welfare of this country depends make it necessary for me to pass on you the sentence required by those laws.[6]

On March 24, Owen's Grand National Union organised a meeting of protest in which Dr Arthur S. Wade D.D. and Robert Owen himself took part with the object of inducing the Government to grant a petition for pardon.[7] Various other meetings took place and these culminated in a great demonstration of April 21, at Copenhagen Fields.

On March 26, 1834, Melbourne wrote to Frampton in reply to a letter of March 22 (not published) promising "that immediate measures will be taken for carrying into effect the sentence, lately passed at Dorchester, upon the six individuals convicted of administering Unlawful Oaths".[8]

Melbourne advises cautious policy

On the same day (March 26) Melbourne wrote to Frampton another letter marked "private and confidential" stating:

We have now had experience, very long experience, amongst the manufacturing population, of this evil, with which we are now perhaps destined to contend in the agricultural districts, and the safest course will be to take that experience for our guide. The farmers stand to the labourers in the same relation as the master manufacturers stand to their workmen. The law with respect to both classes is substantially the same. It may be somewhat varied by particular Acts of Parliament, but in general it is the same. By that law whether wise or otherwise Unions and Combinations for the purpose of raising or of lowering wages, provided they do not resort to violence, force, intimidation, illegal oaths or acts in themselves illegal, are legal. Is it possible then for the Government to advise the Magistrates or for the Magistrates to advise the farmers to discharge their men for doing that, which may be not only legal but just and reasonable? Would not the respective parties so acting take upon themselves a great responsibility, incur much odium and subject themselves to observations which it would be difficult to reply to?[9]

This letter shows with sufficient clearness that the Whigs realised that the main purpose and object of the Tolpuddle union was lawful, and that a mere accidental feature of its organisation had been seized on by the Government and the magistrates (who were all landowners or clergymen of the Established Church) as the most convenient pretext for the purpose of destroying the union.

VI

What the magistrates did

On March 27, Melbourne wrote to Frampton stating that it appeared probable that upon the re-assembling of Parliament "much observation will be made upon the sentence". He asked Frampton to furnish any information that he could as to the six individuals concerned. On March 29, Frampton replied by letter. He said that the farmers "will show a great unwillingness to employ those who are known to have belonged to the Union, without any communications of the Justices on the subject".[1]

Frampton proceeded to give the required particulars. In reference to the two brothers Loveless it was said that they "were very active in the riots in the winter of 1830". Frampton emphasised that the two brothers Loveless and the Standfields father and son were all Methodists and that three of the four were Methodist preachers. He reported of Standfield, the father, that "he is a Labourer, a very discontented man, and if any disturbance is going on he is sure to be in it".[2] Of Standfield the son he said, "Very saucy and ready for any disturbance".[3] The letter added:

> The conviction and prompt execution of the sentence of transportation has given the greatest satisfaction *to all the Higher classes*, and will, I have no doubt, have a very great effect amongst the Labourers; as great pains have been taken to instil into their minds that the men would undergo only a slight punishment; as the Unions were so powerful the Government would not venture to put the Sentence in force.[4]

This was a particularly cunning letter. Frampton refrained from directly requesting Melbourne not to allow any mitigation of the sentences but insinuated that the Government was expected by the employing classes to treat the question of sentence as a contest between the Government and unions, in which any mitigation would be regarded by the public as a victory for the latter. Incidentally it may be noted that, in his pamphlet, George Loveless gave an absolute denial to the suggestion that he was one of the rioters of 1830.[5]

Frampton and the magistrates

It was alleged by Dr Wakley and never directly denied by the magistrates that the six prisoners

> on their arrival were examined by the Magistrates and remanded to the gaol. The next morning the Magistrates actually, instead of bringing them into open Court, visited them in gaol, took the remainder of their depositions in private, and made out their commitment in the gaol. Even the witnesses were committed to gaol in order that they might be compelled to give the required evidence at the trial of the accused. And who was the chief witness whom it was necessary to imprison in order to secure his testimony? Why, the son of the gardener who was in the employment of that very Magistrate who caused the labourers to be apprehended – in fact the whole matter looked like a conspiracy to entrap the accused.[6]

It is suggested by Firth and Hopkinson that neither Williams nor Lord Melbourne was as blameworthy as the magistrates, and that

> the real villains of the piece were Frampton and his fellow squires. They instigated the prosecution, they marked down the victims, they worked on the fear of the Government and its agents. Frampton, who lived within a few miles of Tolpuddle, must have

known that the employers of the doomed labourers were satisfied with their work and their conduct.[7]

Refusal of parish relief to families

Leaving Judge Williams and Melbourne out of consideration for the moment, there is little or nothing to extenuate in Frampton's persistent venom and hatred, even after his victims had been transported. For instance, on May 3, 1834, he wrote to Viscount Howell, Under-Secretary of State, as follows:

It is perfectly true that I, and the other justices acting with me, re-fused to allow any parochial relief for the wives and families of those convicts; and we gave as our reason for so doing that we had ascertained from the gaoler that they had been supplied by their wives with more food than they could consume during the time they were in gaol, which would have been continued after their conviction had the regulations of the prison allowed it. We also told them that on their husbands entering the Union, the leaders of it engaged to maintain all the families of those who joined the Union for so long a time as they were thrown out of work and deprived of their earnings, in consequence of their be-longing to the Union; and that therefore they ought to apply to those leaders and require them to keep their promise. Our object in doing this was to prove to the labourers that the leaders of the Unions had deceived them if they did not support their families; and if they did maintain them to lessen the funds of the Union at the same time that it relieved the Parish.[8]

In the same letter Frampton stated that the justices had also refused Parish relief to all persons "whose names appeared in the book, which was proved on the trial of the six men to contain a list of those who had taken the illegal oath and had joined the Union".[9]

Discrimination against unionists

And, in the third place, Frampton's letter of May 3 said:

> The Justices have particularly recommended to the farmers (who
> have expressed themselves most willing to follow our advice) that
> every encouragement should be given to those labourers who did
> not join the Union by increasing their wages and placing them in
> all the most profitable work, so that they may feel the advantage
> of their good conduct by making a marked difference between
> them and the Unionists; and on no account at present to make
> any addition to the wages of the latter, lest it should have the
> slightest appearance of being done thro' fear.[10]

The conclusion from the correspondence

The documents and facts which have already been summarised make
it clear that the magistrates under Frampton actively organised the
prosecution in collaboration with the Home Office under Lord Melbourne.[11] The "vindictive motives and temper" of the prosecution were
emphasised by Mr Clynes, who rightly stressed the importance of the
recently revealed correspondence between Melbourne, Frampton and
Portman.[12] This correspondence justified Citrine's conclusion that
there was "[a] detestable conspiracy between the Home Secretary and
the Magistrates to bring these poor simple labourers within the clutch-
es of the law", so long as it is remembered that a vindictive
administration of the law for political ends has not yet been held to be
an "unlawful" conspiracy.[13]

VII

Part played by the juries

To the Grand Jury had been assigned the preliminary task of finding a True Bill. We have already noticed that William Ponsonby, Whig M.P. for Dorset and a wealthy landowner, was anxious to take a prominent part on this jury. He was attacked by Wakley (the Radical M.P. for Finsbury) in the latter's important speech in the House of Commons on June 25, 1835.[1] On April 3, Ponsonby, upon returning to London after the trial, impressed on Charles Greville that the sentence must not be interfered with or relaxed in any way "because the lower and labouring classes had their eyes fixed on the case, and an example was needed to stem the demoralisation of Dorsetshire life".[2]

It has also been noted that the Grand Jury included four of the nine justices who had issued the caution of February 22, 1834.[3] Both James and Henry Frampton sat and Ponsonby acted as foreman. Baron Williams addressed them and said:

> He believed that of all persons affected by it, the unfortunate persons themselves who were brought into any state of this kind, and had an oath of this sort administered to them were affected the most. Sure he was, that within his own experience he had known that they had been compelled by the force of an oath, to make out of their scanty means such a large and ample contribution as would not be endured by any class of men to the constituted authorities of the country, or the maintenance of the Government itself. That there had been instances of the grossest oppression by demands made on these persons which were unknown in this

country, but above all, where men were included in Societies of this kind, the common right obligation of every man of labouring as he pleases, and for whom he pleases, was taken away from him, and there was even danger of life and limb attending that person the moment he incurred the displeasure of the party to whom he had subjected himself, of the self-elected persons to whom he pledged his subjection by the oath he had taken.[4]

Is it surprising that the Jury at once returned a True Bill?

The petty jury

Wakley's assertion with reference to the election of the petty jurors, who consisted solely of landowners, was:

> The proceedings connected with their commitment and trial were equally unfair. On the Sunday before the trial an officer connected with the County Court visited Tolpuddle and other neighbouring villages in order to make enquiries relative to the characters of the individuals who were to be summoned as jurors on the trial of the labourers, and the neighbours were asked who would be safe to put into the Jury Box on that occasion. In pursuance of the objects sought to be obtained by this unjust inquisition a tradesman by the name of Bridle, a linen-draper at Bere Regis, was challenged by the Crown and turned out of the jury box, his disqualifying offences being that he was not a farmer, and that he had occasionally heard one of the Lovelesses, two of whom were among the six convicted men, preach in the Methodist Chapel of Bere Regis.[5]

This charge was never falsified. In their study of the case Firth and Hopkinson state that the jury at the trial considered the matter "for five minutes only".[6]

Option to proceed summarily not exercised

The offence of belonging to a society whose members were bound by an oath not to reveal the society's secrets could have been prosecuted summarily under 39 George III, C. 79. Sec. 8 of that Act gave the authorities the alternative of such summary prosecution or proceeding upon indictment. In the former case the penalty was three months' imprisonment or a fine of £20, in the latter case, transportation for any time not exceeding seven years or imprisonment for any time not exceeding two years. This fact was stressed by Wakley who said:

> Yet the illegality of the association was the foundation, in all the counts of the indictment, for sustaining the allegations with regard to the illegality of the oath. Had the indictment been framed in accordance with the spirit and the letter of an Act passed in the 39th of George III – avowedly framed for the purpose of putting down all secret associations, with the exception of the Society of Freemasons and two or three other societies therein specifically named – then indeed, doubts might justly have been entertained whether these men had not offended against the conditions of that Statute, notwithstanding the repeal of the combination laws. But there was a motive for not prosecuting them under that Statute. The poor fellows might then have been proceeded against summarily before the Magistrate and been committed to prison for three months for taking an oath not required or authorised by law, whereas under the 37th George III the Judge upon the conviction of the accused had the power of transporting them for the term of seven years – a power which he could not exceed, and which in the discharge of his duty, he exercised to the very utmost.[7]

Certainly, if it had been desired to make it known that a trade union could not lawfully be conducted if the ceremony of initiating its members included a paraphernalia of oaths of secrecy, the law of the land could have been amply vindicated by a summary prosecution under 39 George III, C. 79. But the clear object of the prosecutors was, not that trade unions should be organised in the manner permitted or at least not prohibited by law, but that they should not operate at all, despite the repeal of the Combination Acts.

VIII

An account of the evidence

I am of opinion that the evidence against the prisoners was sufficient, if true, to support the verdict and finding of the jury. According to Moody and Robinson's report:

> It was proved that Edward Legg was, with other persons, taken by two of the prisoners to a house in the village of Tolpuddle, belonging to a third prisoner, and that there by night, in the presence of all the prisoners, one of whom was dressed in a surplice, a form of words was addressed to them while kneeling down and their eyes bandaged. These words, which imported a dire imprecation on themselves if they revealed what they there saw or heard, they were desired to repeat, and did repeat, after the person pronouncing them; as to whom, evidence was given for the purpose of showing that it was the same prisoner who wore the surplice. After repeating the words, Legg and the others were successively made to kiss a book, which, on their being unblinded, appeared to them like a small Bible, and they were then told that they were all brethren. The representation of a figure of death was exhibited to Legg and the others in the midst of the above ceremony, the bandage being for that purpose removed from their eyes; and one of the prisoners at the same time pronounced the words, 'Remember thy end'.

The association to which these persons were thus admitted was proved to be formed for the purpose of raising wages by a general strike on the part of its members, and for other purposes in furtherance of that design.[1]

The evidence for the prosecution

According to Carrington and Payne:

> A witness named Lark, who was a labourer, said: One of the prisoners, whose name is Brine, came to me while I was threshing, and persuaded me to go to Tolpuddle. I went to the prisoner Thomas Stanfield's [sic] house, upstairs. While he was there, the prisoner John Stanfield [sic] came in; he asked if we were ready all: Some one answered that we were; and he said, then, blind our eyes. We all then tied our handkerchiefs round our eyes, and, being thus blindfolded, we were led into another room, where something was read to us by some person I did not know. I think, from the reading of it, it was out of the Bible; I don't recollect any part of it. We then knelt down, when a book was put into our hands, and an oath administered to us. I don't recollect what the oath was about. We then rose up and were unblinded, when the picture of death, or a skeleton, was shown to us, upon which the prisoner James Lovelass [sic] said, 'Remember your end!' We were then blinded again, and again knelt down, when something was read out of a paper, but what that was I don't remember. I kissed a book when I was unblinded first. I saw George Lovelass [sic] dressed in white; he had on him something like a parson's surplice. Something was said about the rules of the society and about paying one shilling on admission. I saw all the prisoners there when I was unblinded.

Another witness, the informer Edward Legg, said:

> I went with the last witness; they told us something about striking, or that they meant to strike, and that we might do the same if we like. There was nothing said about the time when we should strike. There was something said about our masters having notice

of it, but I don't remember anything about it. We kissed a book when we were blinded. When we were on our knees, we repeated something that was said by somebody, but who said it I don't know. I believe it was like the voice of James Lovelass [sic]. I think the words which we repeated were something about being plunged into eternity, and about keeping secret what was done by the society. I don't know what book it was that I kissed. When I was unblinded I saw a book on the table that resembled a Testament. They shewed us the picture of death, and one of them said, 'Remember your end'.

The rules of the society

It was proved that in a box belonging to the prisoner James Lovelass [sic] was found a book which was headed "General Rules". The first rule was "That this society be called 'The General Society of Labourers'". The substance of the rules was that there should be a lodge in every parish, a committee, a grand lodge, and contributions to support those who quit their work when desired by the grand lodge. That no person should turn out for an advance of wages without the consent of the grand lodge. That no member of the society should work along with any man who acted contrary to any rule prescribed by the grand lodge. That if any man divulged any of the secrets of the society, his name and description should be sent round to all the lodges, and all members should decline to work with him. That no person should be admitted to their meetings when drunk; that no obscene songs or toasts should be allowed; and that they should not countenance any violence or violation of the laws of the realm.[2]

The charge of Williams to the jury

Baron Williams in summing up said:

> If you are satisfied that an oath, or obligation tantamount to an oath, was administered to either of the witnesses Legg or Lock by

means of the prisoners, you ought to find them guilty. The prisoners are indicted under the stat. 37 Geo. III c. 123, the preamble of which refers to seditious and mutinous societies; but I am of opinion that the enacting part of the statute extends to all societies of an illegal nature; and the second section of the stat. 39 Geo. III, c. 79 enacts that all societies shall be illegal, the members of which shall, according to the rules thereof, be required to take an oath or engagement not required by law. If you are satisfied from the evidence respecting the blinding, the kneeling, and the other facts proved, that an oath or obligation was imposed on the witnesses or either of them you ought to find the prisoners guilty; and if you come to that conclusion, I wish you to state whether you are of opinion that the prisoners were united in a society.[3]

According to another report, Williams

concluded by telling the jury that, if they found that such an obligation as was intended to operate as an oath, had been administered by the prisoners, and taken by Legg; if they were of opinion that the oath thus tendered and taken was meant to prohibit him from disclosing what he himself, or others, had done or might do in the society; and if they were also of opinion that the prisoners, as members of the society, had taken a similar oath of secrecy themselves, in that case they should pronounce a verdict of guilty, and accompany their verdict with a special finding as to the latter point.[4]

The jury included in their verdict a special finding "that at the time of administering the oath the prisoners themselves belonged to a secret society, having taken oaths not to disclose the secrets of that society".[5]

Was the secret oath the regular procedure?

It might possibly have been argued that the evidence was insufficient to prove that the ritual of the secret oath was a usual part of its procedure. But there was evidence which might have satisfied an impartial jury that the ritual was adopted in the case of Lark and Legg only because it was according to the regular practice and rule of the union. A suggestion that the Bible and the picture of death were used only for the initiation of these two particular men could hardly have been entertained. As we know, the secret oath was a typical device then adopted by trade unions as well as by the Orange Lodges and Freemasons. Mr Clynes commented:

> Workmen were prevented from speaking or acting in the open in defence of the humblest livelihood. They were thereby driven to secret processes, and they had no choice but to take an oath as others did to indicate their resolve and to avow their regard for the truth.[6]

An opposing point of view, which also shows the existing practice, was expressed in the *Law Magazine* of the day. It asserted that the method of administering oaths was well known by trade unionists to be unlawful, "hence the secrecy, the solemnity, the midnight horrors and the general character pervading their whole proceedings".[7]

James Hammett

At this time, accused persons were unable to give evidence on their own behalf. This probably led to the wrongful conviction of James Hammett, for, in his pamphlet, George Loveless reiterates that James Hammett was not present at the meeting of December 9, as to which the incriminating evidence was given.[8] It seems quite likely that the informers made an error which cost James Hammett very dear.

IX

Were the convictions bad?

The main legal question remains whether, even assuming that the evidence supported the jury's finding, the facts so found amounted to an offence punishable under 37 George III, C. 123. Counsel for the prosecution pointed out quite clearly that he relied principally upon those counts of the indictment "in which the matter charged as intended to be concealed was the very combination itself in which the prisoners were associated together".[1] It will be observed that, inter alia, sec. I of 37 George III, C. 123 penalised the administration of a secret oath not to reveal or discover "any unlawful combination of confederacy". The prosecutor had therefore to prove that the union, as actually administered, should be regarded as constituting such an unlawful combination; and he attempted to do so by proving that the ritual of the oath was a characteristic and essential part of the union's organisation. This attempt of the prosecutor was based upon the terms of 39 George III, C. 79, sec. 2 of which made a combination "unlawful" if, according to its rules or any agreement of its members, the latter took an oath, "not required or authorized by Law".

Unfairness of invoking the Act of 1797

From the point of view of common justice and fairness, the real objection to the introduction of 37 George III, C. 123, was that, as we have seen, section 8 of 39 George III, C. 79 made participation in the combinations made unlawful by that Statute, an offence which could have been punished in a summary way before a Justice of the Peace, or by way of indictment as a misdemeanour instead of as a felony.[2] By the combining of the two Acts originally passed for two different purposes, the prosecution succeeded, firstly, in making the labourers liable to be convicted of felony and transported "for any term of years not exceeding seven years" and, secondly, they excluded the possibility of proceeding under the Act of 39 George III, C. 79 to an infinitely milder form of punishment. The Government deliberately selected the drastic remedy under 37 George III, C. 123. At the least, this was an abuse of the spirit and intent of the latter statute which expressly recited the attempts at mutiny in the Army and Navy in 1797. Further, sec. 7 of 37 George III, C. 123, which was not referred to at the trial of the labourers, provided that any person proceeded against thereunder, whether acquitted or convicted, "shall not be liable to be indicted prosecuted or tried again for the same offence or fact as high treason, or misprision of high treason". The recital and section 8 show that, historically speaking, 37 George III, C. 123 was intended to be applied, and limited, to cases "of a treasonable nature".[3] Instead of that, the Statute was applied to a case where the moral offence was negligible, and no element of treason, or mutiny or sedition or even violence was ever suggested.

Legal objection based on Preamble of 1797 Act

The legal points argued by Counsel for the accused were three in number. The first was that the Statute of 37 George III, C. 123 was limited to the purposes mentioned in its own preamble i.e. mutinous and seditious combinations which had engaged in administering oaths for the purpose of carrying out the purposes of such combination. This argument was rejected by Williams B., and his decision is supported by three precedents. In *R. v Marks,* Lawrence J. said:

> It is true that the preamble and the first part of the enacting clause are confined in their objects to cases of mutiny and sedi-

tion; but it is nothing unusual in Acts of Parliament for the enacting part to go beyond the preamble. The remedy often extends beyond the particular act or mischief which first suggested the necessity of the law; and here the latter part of the clause is conceived in general terms, without any work or reference to the immediate objects of mutiny or sedition before mentioned.[4]

In *Rex v Brodribb* the prisoner was indicted under 37 George III, C. 123 for administering an unlawful oath to sixteen persons, who had been sworn by him to secrecy before they went out armed for the purpose of night poaching.[5] It was argued "that, as the preamble of the statute refers only to meetings for mutinous and seditious purposes, no oaths are within its prohibition, except those administered with some mutinous or seditious object, which was not the case here".[6] But Holroyd J., "without hearing the counsel for the prosecution, overruled the objection".[7] Accordingly the headnote correctly states that "the provisions of the stat. 37 George III, C. 123, which make it a felony to administer an unlawful oath, are not confined to oaths administered with either a mutinous or a seditious object".[8] In *R. v Dixon,* a case tried before Bosanquet J. on July 23, 1834 (after the Dorchester case), which dealt with members of the Cambridge trade union of Operative Cordwainers, the trial judge indicated that he would support Williams' ruling.[9] But the prosecutor had announced that, "as the union was dissolved, he should offer no evidence on this indictment" and a verdict of not guilty was returned accordingly.[10]

Legal objection as to absence of specific oath

The second legal objection was that it had not been proved that a specific oath had been administered, in other words "something has been said about eternity, but the witnesses know not what".[11] But Williams rightly left the jury to decide whether they should infer from the blinding, kneeling and other mumbo-jumbo that the oath was meant to oblige its taker not to disclose the affairs of the society. This ruling is supported by the cases of *R. v. Moors*, and *R. v. Brodribb*.[12] In the latter case, Holroyd J. said: "if the oath administered by the prisoner to the poachers was intended to make the people believe themselves under an engagement, it is equally within the Act whether the book made use of was a Testament or not".[13]

Objection as to absence of unlawful character of union

The third and only formidable objection raised was that the confederacy of the accused was not for an illegal purpose, "the Combination Laws having been repealed, and associations for the purpose of raising wages having no longer a character of illegality impressed upon them".[14]

The contention really amounted to this; because members of trade unions were by the Act of 1825 relieved from being liable to punishment in respect of their meeting specifically for trade union purposes, their exemption from liability extended to all the purposes of the union whatever ritual or mode or organisation and procedure was adopted.

The case of *R. v. Brodribb*, though supporting Williams' rulings upon the two arguments already examined, does not bear at all upon his ruling that a trade union became an illegal combination under 39 George III, C. 79 if its members were required to take an oath not to reveal its secrets and affairs. In *R. v. Brodribb* the prisoner was convicted under 37 George III, C. 123, but the prosecution found the illegal character of the combination or enterprise, not in the fact that its *modus operandi* included the administration of secret oaths, but in the fact that the sixteen persons concerned were going out armed, and with faces disguised, for the purpose of night poaching. As Holroyd J. said:

> As to the assembly itself, and its object, it is impossible that a meeting to go out with faces thus disguised, at night, and under

such circumstances, can be any other than an unlawful assembly; in which case, the oath to keep it secret, is an oath prohibited by this statute. If to go out in such a manner be not indictable as a conspiracy, it is clearly an offence visitable by penalties; perhaps it may even be indictable as a riot. It is not, however, necessary to determine that question now; because it is beyond all doubt an assembly for the purpose of an illegal act.[15]

Williams' ruling followed

On July 23, 1834, Williams' main ruling was followed by Bosanquet J. in *R. v. Dixon*. The latter said:

> I now declare, that all who engage in associations, the members of which, in consequence of being so, take any oaths not required by law, are guilty of an offence against the statute, which, if clearly proved, would, upon conviction, be in every case followed by exemplary punishment. It is impossible that any well-ordered state of society could tolerate the existence of confederacies bound together by secret compacts and oaths not required by law; one of the obvious consequences of such confederacies being to deprive the state of the benefit of the testimony of those who are engaged in them – a state of things injurious to individuals, subversive of public order, and striking at the very existence of the state, by withdrawing the allegiance of the subject from the laws of the land to the secret tribunals of unlawful societies, constraining the conscience by oaths, and seeking to obtain their objects, whatever they might be, by popular intimidation.[16]

Summary of legal position

The legal position may now be expressed as follows. By the Statute 37 George III, C. 123, the administration of an oath not to reveal any unlawful combination was a felony, and those guilty of such administration could be transported for any term of years not exceeding seven. Subsequently by 39 George III, C. 79 (passed in consequence of the activities of the "Corresponding Societies") it was provided that any society then or thereafter established whereby, according to the rules or any agreement of its members, persons were required to take an oath not required or authorised by law, became "unlawful combinations and conspiracies". By sec. 5 of this second statute, an exemption was created in favour of lodges of Freemasons formed under certain conditions including registration.

Reading the two Acts together, it is reasonably clear that, provided the combination or society or union was such that its existing and intending members were bound to take an oath not authorised by law, the society or combination, though otherwise perfectly lawful, became unlawful. If, in addition to this, it was proved that the oath administered bound the taker thereof not to reveal or disclose the existence of the unlawful combination, that is, of the combination or society whose affairs were conducted in such a way that the taking of unauthorised oaths was obligatory, the provisions of 37 George III would become operative against those administering such oaths.

The legal draftsman of the indictment

The form of the relevant counts of the indictment was clearly based upon the above reasoning. Who was the author of the indictment? Sir Walter Citrine states that it was prepared by "one of the supporters of the Government, Sergeant Wilde M.P., the Whig member for Newark".[17]

It is true that, as Wilde stated to the Commons on June 28, 1835, he prepared the indictment on behalf of the Government.[18] But Wilde was not in Parliament in the year 1834, having been defeated by Gladstone for the then "rather rotten borough" in December 1832, and not regaining his seat until the general elections in January 1835, following upon the dismissal of the Melbourne Ministry by William IV.[19] Wilde is accurately described by Morley "as a lawyer of merit and eminence who eighteen years later went to the Woolsack as Lord Truro".[20] It is a very curious fact that the indictment, which (after the prevailing fashion) contained no less than twelve counts, refers the commission of the offence to February 24, 1834, whereas the offence proved by the prosecution related to the previous December. February 24 was the day of the arrest.

X

Opinions as to the legal position

Sir Stafford Cripps' view on the main question of law is that possibly the trial miscarried because of the failure of all concerned to take sufficiently into account the changes in the law brought about by the Acts in 1824 and 1825. As I have shown, the law relied upon by the prosecution required the reading together of the two Acts of 1797 and 1799. It is clear that membership and operation of a trade union, so long as it retained the character of a combination to raise the wages and improve the conditions of its members, were no longer punishable after the passing into law of sec. 4 of the Act of 1825. By that Act, punishment was provided for cases of any violence, threats or intimidation which might be associated with trade union activity, but the penalty for the specific offence was limited to two months' imprisonment. Sir Stafford Cripps' main view is that

> it can never have been intended that a combination legal in itself should have been rendered illegal by the taking of an oath against which there was no prohibition in the Act legalizing the combination. This is, however, a typical case where the actual words of the earlier Statutes were wide enough to give the Court the opportunity, if it so desired, of bringing the acts of the accused within the letter of the law.[1]

Opinion of Sir Stafford Cripps

Sir Stafford Cripps appears however to be emphasising the actual "intention" of the legislators rather than the legal effect of the words used by Parliament. The actual intent, with which one is concerned as historian only, of Peel and Huskisson in 1825, was to go as far as possible towards re-enacting the Combination laws. Hume and Place who opposed themselves to this attempt were more successful in their opposition than at one time seemed likely.[2] But the language used in the Act of 1825 makes it difficult to adopt the suggestion that all trade union activities whatsoever were legalised except so far as the Act made express provision for punishment.[3]

It follows that the Acts of 1824 and 1825 could not operate as an implied repeal in respect of trade unions, only of the provisions of the Acts of 1797 and 1799 dealing with unlawful oaths. The Acts of 1824 and 1825 were not at all concerned with the question of secret or unauthorised oaths, nor were they intended to be a complete and exhaustive code of everything which persons combined in trade associations might or might not lawfully do.

Law Magazine upholds Williams' law

Much the same opinion was expressed at the time by the *Law Magazine*. The general attitude of its controllers to trade unionism was hostile, as witness its assertion:

> The trades' unions are legally constituted with reference to one object, the raising the rate of wages. But this object, unfortunately, cannot be obtained (as all experience shows) without a system of intimidation dangerous and mischievous in principle and too frequently carried into effect through the daily perpetration of acts of illegal violence. Hence the necessity of secret oaths and the mummery of initiation, in order to bind together ignorant men, by the influence of terror, to the commission of acts of persecution from which each would individually shrink.[4]

But the more reasoned and less political portion of the article is convincing enough. It pointed out that evidence proving the administration of an oath of secrecy to persons admitted to a combination

> has a double effect. It proves first, the administering of an oath; secondly, the unlawful nature of the combination, *because* it sanctions the administering of an oath not required or authorised by law. It is not with administering an oath not required or authorised by law that the Dorsetshire labourers stood charged, as still seems to be imagined by the leaders of the unions, if we may judge of the words of the petition of last Monday; but with the administering of an oath not to reveal a combination which administers such oaths.[5]

In special reference to the trial the article said:

> All that it was necessary to prove in the Dorsetshire case was the administering of an oath of secrecy, and this was done by the testimony of the two approvers and the existence of a society into which the persons sworn were admitted, and this was done by the same testimony, and by the production of the rules of the society in question.[6]

So definite and dogmatic was the view taken by the *Law Magazine* that it said:

> We cannot seriously expect that any well supported attempt will be made to prove that the Dorchester conviction was not within the *letter* and legal spirit of the Statutes.[7]

Hurst's view

Sir Gerald B. Hurst, in his article in the *English Historical Review*, points out that *Rex v. Loveless* has been regarded by legal text writers as deciding

(1) that, notwithstanding the preamble to the Unlawful Oaths Act of 1797, the Statute was not limited to Oaths administered for the purpose of mutiny or sedition.

(2) That every association, the members of which were bound by oath not to reveal its secrets, was unlawful in the absence of a definite Statute to the contrary, whatever was the purpose of the association and

(3) the administration of an oath not to reveal anything done by such an association was an offence against the Act of 1797.[8]

Hurst states that the decision "is still regarded as a good authority on the true interpretation of the Unlawful Oaths Act 1797", and that the conviction of the six labourers "appears to have been warranted by the language of the Unlawful Oaths Act, for it is still treated as a good authority in modern text books on criminal law".[9] Although the reference to the acceptance in text-books on criminal law of mere decisions of single Judges at *nisi prius* is not in itself conclusive, it seems that the conclusion of Hurst should be accepted. Therefore, J.L. Hammond is correct in saying: "Unhappily, though trade unions were no longer illegal, these oaths were".[10]

Here we may note Sir Stafford Cripps' reference to the failure of the authorities to prosecute those who conducted the Orange Lodges and made use of the instrument of the oath of secrecy: "it is beyond doubt that in such a case as the Orange oath no prosecution was ever launched; had it been there is little doubt that the trial would have ended in an acquittal, for the Orange Societies offered no challenge to the dominant class".[11] It must also be remembered that subject to certain restrictions secret oaths were expressly permitted in relation to Freemasons' Lodges.[12]

XI

Judge Williams and the sentences

As Sir John Williams was appointed Baron of the Exchequer on February 28, 1834, the trial of the labourers came before him in the course of his first Assizes. It is said in the *Dictionary of National Biography* of Williams that, "as a Judge, Williams was painstaking and conscientious, and appeared to special advantage in criminal cases".[1] On the other hand Firth and Hopkinson declare that "Williams was an instrument of the Whig Policy of repression".[2] Hurst's view is that

> there is little to challenge in his conduct of the proceedings or his interpretation of the law. It is rather his conception of the offence and of its proper penalty which excited the wrath of many of his own generation and provokes the horror of ours.[3]

Sir Stafford Cripps however strongly criticises Williams' conduct of the trial, saying "the Judge's conduct was grossly irregular and he constituted himself a violent advocate for the prosecution, in his determination to secure a conviction".[4] He supports this criticism by a reference to certain statements in the *Law Magazine*.[5] For instance he quotes the following statement:

> the evidence, which was drawn from them with the utmost reluctance and by severe questioning, did not at all equal in amount (though it did not contradict) that which they had before voluntarily given. No one who saw their demeanour could doubt that they were under the influence of terror or of some sinister motive.[6]

But the writer of the *Law Magazine* article went on to add:

> Under such circumstances, it would unquestionably have been within the Judge's authority, perhaps a part of his duty, to have pressed a witness to further disclosure by reminding him of his former statements. It seemed to be the general opinion at the trial that this power was too sparingly exercised. Yet, overcautious as the learned Judge perhaps was in this respect, we understand that the few questions put by him have been made the foundation of a charge, and that the ignorant hearers or readers of his accusers' declamations have been assured that the witnesses were unfairly led into the important disclosures which secured the conviction![7]

The suggestion of unfair intervention on Williams' part does not find any real support in the contemporary article which suggests that Williams was *too* considerate. The other sources relied upon by Sir Stafford Cripps are a letter from a barrister quoted by O'Connell during a Commons debate and Loveless' own account of the trial as published in his *Victims of Whiggery*.[8]

Sir Stafford Cripps' criticism that Williams' conduct "was grossly irregular" cannot be accepted without considerable qualification. But his opinion that the punishment inflicted was because of the purpose of the trade union, not the mere taking of an oath of secrecy as part of its procedure, is unanswerable.

Williams tries another case

On July 28, 1834, Williams, now promoted to be a Justice of the King's Bench instead of an Exchequer Baron, presided at another trial for administering an unlawful oath.[9] The trade union concerned consisted mainly of women engaged in button-making; and the ritual was referred to at length in the depositions. For instance one deponent said:

> Previously to going into the room, a woman, whom I did not know, bound my eyes with a handkerchief, and led me to a large

dining-table in the club-room. We all knelt down, and had our right hands on the left breast, and the left hands on the Bible. We solemnly declared we would not make buttons under 6d. or 10d.; that we would keep all the secrets of the lodge, and never give our consent that any of the money should be divided or appropriated to any other purpose than the use of the union; if we did, might our souls drop into the bottomless pit. One of the prisoners then said, 'Now, sisters, you are members of our honourable society, and may you ever prove worthy of the honour conferred upon you.[10]

The prisoners pleaded guilty, and Williams said:

I am bound to say that, having read the depositions, I do not entertain a particle of doubt that provided the fact there disclosed had been proved against you, it was an offence within the statutes; and I believe that no man, who has the fairness or industry to peruse those Acts of Parliament, and to understand them, can entertain a doubt that, to administer an oath or engagement not to reveal the secrets of any association, is within the stat. 37 Geo. III c. 123 as explained and modified by subsequent statutes – I say that it is within the meaning of those statutes, not as has been ignorantly supposed or represented, because it had reference to any matter respecting wages; but on the ground that every association of that kind, bound together by an oath not to disclose the proceedings of that Society, is for that reason, and not for the other, an unlawful combination within the meaning of the statutes of the realm.[11]

This ruling is in strict accordance with the Dorchester decision. But the sentence imposed was very different for the prisoners were all discharged on their own recognisances, to appear to receive judgment when called on. This case rather suggests that although Williams' law was sound (Sergeant Ludlow appeared for the prisoners who pleaded guilty in Ball's case), his terrible Dorchester sentence was, to some extent, repented of. Indeed the trade union in question (in *R. v. Ball*) was conducted with much more vigour and activity than the pathetic lodge at Tolpuddle.

The sentence of seven years transportation

In his pamphlet George Loveless refers to "the cruel sentence of a Whig Judge (Baron John Williams) ... this man has earned an ignoble fame".[12] Nothing can justify the condemnation of these labourers to transportation beyond the seas. Loveless said: "I would assure Lord Stanley who boasted a few years since that he would make transportation worse than death that his cruel and diabolical purpose is more than accomplished".[13] Indeed the usual effect of such a sentence was correctly, if brutally, described by Baron Alderson in 1831, when he administered a similar sentence.[14]

> You will leave the country ... you will see your friends and relations no more: for though you will be transported for seven years only, it is not likely that at the expiration of that term you will find yourselves in a situation to return. You will be in a distant land at the expiration of your sentence. The land which you have disgraced will see you no more: the friends with whom you are connected will be parted from you forever in this world.

All must agree that the sentence was cruelly unjust and disproportionate. Laski says: "The sentence imposed was monstrous".[15] The Webbs describe it as "ferocious" and "barbarous", and mainly for that reason, denounce the trial as a "scandalous perversion of the law".[16]

The protests against the sentence

The protests against the carrying out of the sentence came from many parts of England, and they were not entirely limited to the working class bodies. The general character of the appeals for clemency is illustrated by Wakley's speech of June, 1835.

He implored the House, he entreated the noble Lord to take this fitting opportunity of extending mercy to the men, thereby gratifying thousands of the labouring classes who had appeared before the House as petitioners. Enough had already been done to deter others from following their example, and there was no longer reason why mercy should not be extended to these poor men. He lamented that the labouring classes had no representatives in the House. He had no desire to press the motion to a division; he hoped the noble lord would see the propriety of bringing the men back to their country. The people of England, he could assure the House, felt deeply on the subject. To the working classes especially it was a constant subject of agitation, and unless the men were restored that agitation would continually increase. The society was legal with the single exception of the oath; and when the object was legal the oath alone could not make the society illegal. He hoped the House would interpose its authority. [17]

A similar attitude was adopted by many of the newspapers. On March 28, 1834, the *Standard* (Tory) newspaper said: "But let those who have sinned in ignorance have the benefit of that ignorance; let the six poor Dorsetshire fellows be restored to their cottages".[18] On 29 March 1834, the *Morning Post* (Whig) said:

> the Dorchester conspirators were, we admit, as little dangerous as it is possible for conspirators to be. The Trades Unions are, we have no doubt, the most dangerous institutions that were ever permitted to take root, under the shelter of the law, in any country.[19]

The Tory *Morning Herald* said the verdict showed "rather the treachery than the energy of the law by throwing the noose of an Act of Parliament over the heads of sleeping men".[20] Wakley's speech seems to have created a profound impression. Roebuck said that it was a "touching and beautiful appeal to our sympathy and our justice".[21]

XII

Whigs and Tories in agreement

Lord John Russell, the Home Secretary in Melbourne's Ministry, expressed the Government's willingness to recommend to the King a grant of pardon to all except the two brothers Loveless, after the prisoners had remained in Australia for two years. With regard to the two Lovelesses whom he regarded as ringleaders he said they would have to remain in the colonies for the full period of seven years. Wakley's motion was pressed to a division, but was defeated by 308 to 82.[1] The tellers for the motion were Wakley and Joseph Hume. It was supported by Daniel O'Connell, and the 82 supporters comprised 63 Radical-Liberals, 12 Tories and only seven Whigs. On August 12, 1835, Wakley presented a petition from 5000 inhabitants of Bristol, and he "contrasted the punishment inflicted on these unfortunate men with the perfect immunity which members of Orange Lodges enjoyed".[2] On February 23, 1836, Sir William Molesworth supported a motion by Joseph Hume for the suppression of the Orange Lodges, contending that they were far more deserving of punishment than the innocent Dorchester labourers.[3] But it was not until March 14, 1836, that Russell announced that the King had granted a free pardon to all six labourers.[4]

Lord Melbourne and William IV

In considering the position of Melbourne, who was Home Secretary at the time of the conviction, the historian is impeded to some extent by the fact that his published letters do not necessarily give a full transcript, careful editing and economical disclosure being the maxim.[5] For instance, the letter of Melbourne to the Dorset magistrate, James Frampton, of March 26, 1834, marked "private and confidential", omits from the printed record the first, fourth and fifth paragraphs and the existence of these omissions is nowhere indicated.[6] There is no special significance about the omitted portions of this particular letter, but the fact is sufficient to put one on guard against the assumption that the published letters are necessarily complete. It may also be noted that the editor (Sanders) was sufficiently hostile to the Dorsetshire labourers to induce him to regard their hurried transportation after conviction as "a wise precaution".[7]

In his history of the affair, Sir Walter Citrine rightly emphasises the importance of William IV's hostility to the trade unions. The King's letter to Lord Melbourne at the Home Office, dated March 30, 1834, is set out by Citrine in full.[8] But Melbourne's reply to the King is merely summarised.[9] There are several vital phrases in this reply which constitute perhaps the most important piece of evidence as to the Government's policy of suppression.

It has already been noted that Melbourne wrote that, on assuming office in November 1830, Sir Robert Peel had declared that the trade union question constituted "the most formidable difficulty and danger with which we had to contend", an opinion with which the Whig Government obviously concurred.[10] And now, in 1834, Lord Melbourne said of the trade unions, in reply to the King's letter of March 30, 1834:

That they inflict loss both upon those who engage in them and upon those against whom they are directed, both upon the masters and the men, and consequently upon the community at large, is a clear, undeniable fact; but notwithstanding their menacing language and attitude, Viscount Melbourne does not at present anticipate from them any material disturbance of the public peace. Men often threaten the most violently when they are the most afraid, and Viscount Melbourne attributes their present clamour to the strong impression made upon them by the recent conviction in Dorchester, and to their consciousness of *the mortal blow which it strikes at the root of the whole of their proceedings.*[11]

The circumstances in which this blow was aimed and delivered have been described. Impartial historians must condemn Melbourne and the local magistrates out of their own mouths for combining to abuse the proceedings of the courts for the attainment of an illegitimate end; i.e. the suppression of trade unions, however lawfully they might be conducted. The personal hostility of William IV to the trade unions is conclusively evidenced. In his letter of March 30, 1834 to Melbourne, the King attacked the Birmingham unions in particular and said:

> Upon the whole the King cannot lose sight of the importance of endeavouring to impose some check to the *progress* of this evil, and to adopt some *preventive* measures, instead of trusting to its *decay* after the edifice shall have been injured; and he is anxious that the question should be brought under the consideration of his Government at the approaching meeting of Cabinet.[12]

Lord John Russell persuades Melbourne to relent

In June 1834, Melbourne succeeded Grey as Prime Minister, but his Ministry was dismissed by William IV in November, 1834. It was not until April 1835, after the dissolution, that Melbourne regained his position, the elections not giving Peel the majority expected by himself and the King. Lord John Russell became Home Secretary despite the King's strong personal dislike and hostility.

Russell's attitude towards the men was less unfavourable than that of Melbourne.[13] On October 2, 1835 Russell wrote to Melbourne, indicating the he (Russell) had written to the Colonial Office to the effect that the two brothers Loveless should be pardoned after three years in the Colony. He added:

Now Joseph Hume writes me a letter which I send you. I am not disposed myself to do more than I have done, for then we should be in their power, instead of their being in ours. What say you? To be sure the Duke of Cumberland and the Duke of Gordon are far more guilty than the labourers, but the Law does not reach them I fear.[14]

This was a reference to the leaders of the Orange Lodge movement. On 6 October 1835, Melbourne replied:

I am certainly quite against doing anything more in the case of the Dorsetshire labourers. I thought the matter had been considered to have been settled. Perhaps if it will tend to prevent the revival of the question, you might facilitate their being joined by their families.[15]

Russell again wrote to Melbourne, stating that George Loveless had asserted that he did not know that his actions were unlawful, adding:

Now as to the unlawfulness, it required putting together two Acts of Parliament to prove that the thing was unlawful; O'Connell says now that it was lawful and no proclamation warned them that what was notoriously done all over London was illegal. Secondly, it appears that the Duke of Cumberland and Lord Wynford have been doing the same thing only with more cunning, and deserve at least a more severe punishment. I have already offered the wives of the Lovelesses to go out, but they would not go till their husbands were consulted. Certainly if I stay in office I shall not keep the sentence in force the whole seven years.[16]

On 13 October 1835, Melbourne gave way. He wrote to Russell: "I do not myself care much what is done respecting the Dorsetshire labourers. But you know the feeling which exists against their being brought back into the country".[17]

XIII

Treatment of the prisoners in Australia

On April 11, 1834, all the labourers except George Loveless were transported. They arrived in Sydney on August 17, 1834. On May 25, 1834, George Loveless was deported from Spithead, and he arrived in Van Diemen's Land early in September 1834. It has been alleged that Governors Bourke and Arthur, who were administering New South Wales and Van Diemen's Land respectively, were guilty of harsh and oppressive treatment of the six men. George Loveless wrote of the Whig Government:

> Monstrous hypocrites ... to doom them to a species of punishment, which they themselves had boasted to have made worse than death; to keep them in the colonies (or at least look on with indifference while their subalterns so act) after they have granted a free pardon, reluctantly wrung from them, to screen the Duke of Cumberland and his Orange Confederates![1]

Firth and Hopkinson assert that "by deliberate trickery the news of their pardon was kept from them till they had served about two years of their punishment".[2] This assertion is unjustified as will presently appear. They also refer to "the reluctance of the Australian officials to inform the prisoners of their free pardon".[3] The Webbs state that: "Through official blundering it was two years later (April, 1838) before five out of the six prisoners returned home".[4] A close examination of the facts and documents relating to the actions of the Colonial officials does not substantiate these serious charges against Bourke and Arthur.

The dispatches

On June 12, 1835, Lord Glenelg sent a dispatch to Bourke to the effect that, upon certain conditions, he (Bourke) would be authorised to grant a pardon to the five convicts who were then under Bourke's jurisdiction within New South Wales, viz., the two Standfields, Hammett, Brine and James Loveless. This dispatch imposed the condition that the labourers in New South Wales, except James Loveless, should continue to reside there for the term of two years from the date of their arrival, and that James Loveless should continue to reside there during the remainder of the sentence.[5] Sir Walter Citrine says that, according to this dispatch:

> all except James Loveless should have been set at liberty at once, although they would not have been allowed to return to England for a further eight months, as their two years' residence in the Colony did not expire until September, 1836. For some reason however, the authorities were reluctant to liberate them. What was the explanation of this?[6]

As will appear later, it is by no means certain that it was intended by the authorities to alter the colonial status of the men from that of servitude to complete freedom. But Citrine rightly emphasises the importance of the dispatch marked "private and separate" of July 7, 1835, which referred to the Statute 2 William IV, C. 62. And in addition to this "private and separate dispatch", there was an official and open dispatch, also of July 7, 1835, from Glenelg, which stated that Lord John Russell had expressed a doubt as to the legal authority of Bourke to grant the pardon authorised by the dispatch of June 12.

The case of George Loveless, who was in Van Diemen's Land, will be referred to separately. The remaining five labourers had landed in New South Wales by the convict ship *Surry* on August 17, 1834, so that the suggested term of residence for four of them would not elapse until August 17, 1836, and for James Loveless until August 17, 1837.

Bourke had no power to remit sentence

The real difficulty felt by Lord John Russell was occasioned by 2 William IV, C. 62. Section 2 of that Act (passed in July, 1832) had provided as follows:

> That neither the Governor or Lieutenant-Governor of any island, colony, or settlement, or any other person, shall give any pardon or ticket of leave to any person sentenced to transportation, or who shall receive a pardon on condition of transportation, or any order or permission to suspend or remit the labour of any such person, except in cases of illness, until such person, if transported for seven years, shall have served four, if transported for fourteen years, shall have served six, or if transported for life, shall have served eight years of labour.

And the section concluded: "Provided that nothing herein contained shall in any manner affect His Majesty's royal prerogative of mercy."

When, therefore, in his "private and separate" dispatch of July 7, 1835, Lord Glenelg referred to the legal position, he was correct in pointing out that the prisoners, having been sentenced to transportation for seven years, were wholly excluded by the Act of 2 William IV from receiving any indulgence from Bourke himself until after the expiration of four years of the sentence and that any pardon, to be lawful, must be by virtue of a Warrant under the Royal Sign Manual.[7] Certainly, Glenelg desired that leniency should be extended to the five prisoners in New South Wales. But Governor Bourke rightly felt that the command of Section 2 was too strong and clear to disobey, and that the British Government should itself take the responsibility of obtaining the King's own pardon in accordance with the proviso to the section. In substance, as is rightly pointed out by Sir Walter Citrine, Glenelg sought to impose the task "upon Sir Richard Bourke of finding a way round the Act of Parliament".[8] The disinclination of the Melbourne Ministry to approach the King is explained by the latter's vehement hostility to the trade unions, and his proved dislike, and even readiness to dismiss, a Whig ministry. The open dispatch of July 7, 1835, required the Governor to report as early as possible upon the prisoners in New South Wales, with a view to the exercise by the King himself under the Royal Sign Manual of his prerogative of mercy.

The case of James Loveless

In addition to the three dispatches mentioned above (that of June 12, 1835, and the two of July 7, 1835), another dispatch was communicated by Glenelg on August 13, 1835. Therein Glenelg informed Bourke that it should be ascertained whether James Loveless "is anxious that his wife and family should join him in the Colony". Bourke was to report the result of the inquiry, "and if you should be of opinion that the prisoner is deserving of favour, Lord J. Russell has stated his readiness on receiving your recommendation to propose the prisoner's return to this country, before the expiration of his sentence.[9] Subsequently, on October 6, 1835, Lord Glenelg sent a further dispatch referring to James Loveless. He stated that it was the intention of the Home Secretary to recommend the prisoner for a pardon "so as to permit him to return home at the expiration of three years from the date of his arrival at New South Wales provided his conduct shall be found to have been good since his transportation".[10]

Explanation of Bourke's actions

The explanation of Bourke's action in not releasing the other four men in New South Wales, in accordance with the first authorisation in the dispatch of June 12, 1835, is now reasonably clear. A perusal of the records now available at the Mitchell Library at Sydney shows that all three dispatches (the one of June and the other two of July) arrived in New South Wales by the same vessel on October 26, 1835. Having regard to the authoritative reference to the provisions of the disabling Statute, it was impossible for Burke to act upon the original authorisation of June 12, 1835. But he adopted Glenelg's suggestion (in his private and separate dispatch) that all five men should be immediately released from penal labour. Bourke withdrew the men from the masters to whom they had been assigned, and removed them to Port Macquarie. Bourke in his dispatch to England of February 20, 1836, mentioned this fact, and declared that at Port Macquarie the Magistrate would be instructed "to allow them every indulgence consistent with their situation".[11] He also stated that he considered this to be the most convenient way of acting during the time which must elapse before the King's pardon could be received. He added that he had sought to accomplish, "as far as law will admit, the intentions expressed in Your Lordship's several communications regarding these persons".[12]

Explanation of removal to Port Macquarie

Further, as soon as the dispatches arrived in Sydney, Bourke took action for the purpose of making investigation of the character of the men suggested in the open dispatch of July 7, 1835. He directed the Colonial Secretary of the Colony to make the necessary enquiries and, in his dispatch of February 20, 1836, he reported as follows: "I have the satisfaction of stating that the conduct of each of these individuals has been favourably reported".[13] In reference to Bourke's decision to send the prisoners to Port Macquarie, Sir Walter Citrine's comment is: "What he intended to happen to them while they were at the penal settlement, it is impossible to conjecture".[14] But there is no reason to suppose that Bourke had any intention, except that of having the five men at hand so that they could obtain the full benefit of the conditional pardons at the very first moment the law would permit. It is true, as Citrine adds, that the prisoners preferred to return to their former employers rather than remain at Port Macquarie, but this was not the direct responsibility of Bourke, who felt himself bound by the clear letter of the law.

XIV

The pardons

It was not until November 12, 1835 that Glenelg sent his dispatch transmitting the conditional pardons from the King for the five men in New South Wales. The dispatch desired Bourke to "take the necessary measures for ensuring to the prisoners the full benefits thereof as soon as the respective periods fixed in the warrants shall have expired".[1] The dispatch arrived per the ship *Strathfieldsay* on June 15, 1836. On June 17, Bourke communicated the direction and the conditional pardons to his Colonial Secretary. Glenelg's original dispatch to Bourke is minuted with a reference to the direction to the local Colonial Secretary and with the words "No answer", i.e. no formal answer to Bourke from his local Colonial Secretary.[2] But on June 21, 1836, i.e. only six days after the arrival of the dispatch, the local Colonial Secretary (Alexander McLeay) notified in the Government Gazette that Brine, Hammett and the two Standfields had received conditional pardons, the condition being that "of residing in New South Wales for the term of two years from the day of their arrival"; and that James Loveless had received a conditional pardon, the condition being residence in New South Wales for three years from the day of his arrival.

Interpretation of conditional pardons

On June 21 also, the Governor directed his Colonial Secretary to take measures for ensuring the benefit of the pardons to the five men "as soon as the respective periods fixed in the warrants shall have transpired" [sic "expired"?].[3] Here a curious point should be noted. As we have seen, the five labourers had arrived in New South Wales on August 17, 1834, so that the period of residence in the Colony required in the case of James Loveless would not elapse until August 17, 1837, and, in the case of the other four under Bourke's immediate jurisdiction, until August 17, 1836. Copies of the actual warrants evidencing the Royal Pardon are not to be found; but the Gazette notification and Bourke's direction suggest that, as explained, the five labourers were not to take any benefit under the conditions of the pardon until August, 1836, and August, 1837; in other words, that they were not intended to enjoy their freedom (subject only to the condition of residence) before those dates.[4] Bourke's interpretation of the pardons appears from his dispatch to Glenelg of February 20, 1836, where he said:

> As the pardons to be granted to them are intended, as stated by your Lordship, to operate after a residence in the Colony on the part of four of them for two, and on the part of one of them for three years, it may be proper to report that they all arrived here by the ship *Surry* on the 17th August, 1834.[5]

It was not inconsistent with this that the men should be at once released from "service" and that "residence" only should be required, but the interpretation of Bourke appears to have been that service was required until the dates specified. It is clear, however, that George Loveless was released from Government service in Tasmania as early as February 5, 1836.

News of the free pardon

The dispatch from Glenelg forwarding the free pardons is dealt with by Citrine as follows:

> John Standfield wrote to George Loveless in Van Diemen's Land in November, 1837 [sic 1836], and, in the reply which they received from him in January, 1837, he told them that a full pardon

had been granted and informed them how they could secure a free passage home. No word of this pardon had been received by the authorities, although, of course, they must have known about it. It is singular that the dispatch containing this pardon is missing from the historical records of Australia. It is stated there, however, that the news of the free pardon was communicated to the Governor of Australasia, Sir Richard Bourke, in a dispatch from Lord Glenelg, on March 18th, 1836. The authorities must, therefore, have been in full possession of the pardon by August, 1836, and John Standfield immediately wrote to James Loveless, informing him of the good news. [6]

Bourke and the free pardons

The actual facts as to the dispatch communicating a free pardon are as follows. On March 14, 1836, Wakley presented further petitions on behalf of the two Lovelesses when Lord John Russell announced to the Commons that the King had been pleased to grant a free pardon to the whole of the men. The dispatch communicating this decision was dated March 24, 1836, not March 18, 1836. It is correct that the dispatch is not printed in any official records yet published in reference to this part of Australian history, but the dispatch is in existence and may be inspected in the Mitchell Library in Sydney. As appears from its face it did not arrive in Sydney until August 31, 1836, by the Ship *Moffat*. Bourke immediately informed his local Colonial Secretary by a memorandum dated September 4, 1836. Further the names of the five prisoners in New South Wales were all included in the Government Gazette of September 6, 1836, which was published on the following day, September 7. The extract from the Government Gazette containing the particulars of the names of the men pardoned was also published in *The Australian* newspaper on September 13, 1836.

Although, therefore, it is probable that some of the subordinate authorities in New South Wales failed in their duty to carry the good news as speedily as they should, it must be remembered that communication was very difficult and infrequent in the then state of the colony, particularly in the case of remotely situated grazing properties. And there is little or no evidence that Bourke, who was undoubtedly a humane and just administrator, was deserving of blame in relation to the five prisoners under his jurisdiction. Had they chosen to remain at Port Macquarie as Bourke wished, much delay would have been obviated.

George Loveless' treatment

In spite of one or two comments in his pamphlet *The victims of Whiggery*, that pamphlet itself bears internal evidence that Colonel Arthur, the then Governor of Van Diemen's Land, made no attempt whatever to penalise George Loveless. The latter was sent to Hobart Town. From his pamphlet it appears that on January 7, 1836, an enquiry was made by the authorities as to whether his wife and family were desirous of joining him in the Colony. On January 24 the Governor himself discussed the proposal with him. Arthur said: "I would gladly give you indulgence myself but that I dare not, in consequence of an Act of Parliament passed that no seven years man is to obtain a ticket of leave till he has been four years in the colony".[7]

Arthur also told Loveless that he had sent to England a favourable report about his conduct. On February 5, 1836, George Loveless received a "ticket" from the overseer, "exempting him from Government labour, to employ himself to his own advantage until further order".[8] Loveless speaks of this concession as being of little or no value owing to the practical impossibility of obtaining wages from employment as a free man. On September 16, 1836, the Hobart Town *Tasmanian* announced that he had received a free pardon. Loveless got in touch with the authorities who appear not to have known his immediate whereabouts.[9] It may be noted that the *Tasmanian* newspaper stated, in praise of Arthur, that the latter had received "orders … from the Home Government to work the Dorchester Unionists in irons on the roads", but that Arthur would not comply.[10] There is no evidence that such an instruction was ever sent, though it was not unnatural that George Loveless should be ready to believe the probability of such an instruction, and to state it in his pamphlet.

No evidence of victimisation by Colonial Governors

But two points sufficiently emerge. The suggestion of victimisation on the part of Bourke and Arthur is not supported by the facts or the documents. *A priori* participation by either in so wanton an aggravation of the original injury inflicted on the men was very unlikely. The full responsibility for all their sufferings must rest with the authorities in England, and not with their agents and servants in Australia, who are entitled to an acquittal on the charge of being parties to a special victimisation of the labourers. The disinclination of the Melbourne Ministry to approach William IV to obtain the necessary prerogative instrument was the cause of the delay in carrying out the intention to pardon.

As a matter of fact George Loveless did not receive a letter from his wife stating that she was *not* coming to join him until December 23, 1836. He left Van Diemen's Land by the next available vessel on January 30, 1837, arriving in England on June 13, and in August published his *Victims of Whiggery* pamphlet. The explanation of the facts that the two Standfields, James Loveless and Brine did not leave Sydney for England until September 11, 1837, arriving there on March 1, 1838, four years after the trial, and that Hammett did not arrive in England until August 1839, is probably to be found in the remoteness of their place of labour or the disinclination of their masters to inform them of their full rights.

XV

The Church's attitude

George Loveless regarded himself as victimised, in part at least, because he was a Methodist. He characterised the Vicar of Tolpuddle as that "hireling parson".[1] And he asserted; "The secret is this: I am from principle, a Dissenter, and by some, in Tolpuddle, it is considered as the sin of witchcraft; nay, there is no forgiveness for it in this world nor that which is to come: the years 1824–28 are not forgotten".[2]

Certainly the attitude of the Established Church was one of almost uniform hostility to the labourers. That great churchman, Gladstone, in his Newark address in 1832, referred to the need for adequate remuneration of labour, "which, unhappily, among several classes of our fellow workmen is not now the case".[3] But Gladstone did nothing to show the slightest interest in, or concern for, the six men of Dorchester. The local Vicar, Dr Warren, whose services were invoked in order to secure a settlement of the original wage dispute, seems at first to have lent some encouragement to the labourers. But he soon receded from this attitude, much to the disgust of George Loveless and his friends.[4] Most of the men actively concerned in the union were Methodists. The Church authorities busied themselves in obtaining signatures of certain "Church petitions", which were obviously designed to prevent any extension of the union through the County.[5] When the men were in gaol, they received little pity, let alone courtesy, from the Chaplain, Rev. Dacre Clemetson.[6] In the circumstances, we are not overpowered with surprise to find that on April 2, 1834 Frampton informed Melbourne that the windows of the Parsonage House at

Tolpuddle had been broken.[7] With one notable exception, clergymen of the Established Church took no part in the agitation for the remission of the sentence. That exception was Dr Wade, Vicar of St Nicholas, Warwick, "a stalwart figure weighing twenty stones", who was prominent throughout the London agitation for remission of the sentence.[8] Wade's conduct is reminiscent of the charity of Bishop Sumner during the agricultural riots of 1830.[9] "I have at last", said Cobbett, "found a bishop of the Low Church to praise".[10] In connection with the drastic punishments inflicted after the 1830 riots, the Established Church had acted as "the praying section of the Tory party". *The Times* said: "Surely of all classes of society the clergy is that which ought not to be backward in the remission of offences".[11]

The Church in 1834 behaved like the Church in 1830–31. On each occasion, as the Hammonds phrase it, the English Church "kept religion in its place".[12]

XVI

Consequences of the case

The effect of the conviction and punishment of the Dorchester labourers has often been misunderstood. J.G. Greenwood said that "the only result of the prosecution was to cause the Grand National and other large unions to discard the oath from their admission ceremony.[1] And Firth and Hopkinson actually assert that "trade unionism took strides forward as a result of the interest and indignation aroused in the Dorchester trial."[2] But these two statements are quite opposed to the evidence. J.L. Hammond says that: "Melbourne knew that it would be easier to break the spirit of the starving and ill-used men in these villages than those living in towns or combined in some large industry".[3] And he points our correctly that Melbourne "was successful".[4] In the opinion of Hurst:

> The only lasting legacy of the Dorchester labourers was a lesson as to the policy which trade unionists in other parts of the country learnt from their afflictions. From this time they gave up their early attachment to secret oaths and to elaborate ritual.[5]

Hurst also said:

> It cannot, however, be said that the agitation in their favour marked a real step forward in the history of trade unionism. It seems in no way to have hastened the slow movement towards its legal recognition. The belated release of the sufferers led to no local revival of their cause. In 1837, Dorsetshire wages (7/6 a week) were the lowest in England, and for at least two generations af-

terwards the county remained an area where low wages were the rule and where the employed classes continued to be wholly un-organised. Farm workers all over England lost interest in the idea of Combination.[6]

Even the six victimised labourers themselves (except Hammett) left England for Canada in 1844. "It appears that they made a compact amongst themselves that the story should be kept locked in their own breasts".[7] It is quite misleading to suggest that Melbourne's attack was unsuccessful, the contrary is the case. As Mr H.L. Beales points out:

> When Lord Melbourne struck at village Trade Unionism, by the prosecution of the Tolpuddle labourers, he destroyed more than he knew. Social justice cannot come from above. It must be built up by free men in co-operation. He crippled for a generation the agencies of construction and confined the ideal of self-help within the strait-waistcoat of mean Victorian thrift.[8]

Supposed effect of case on Parliamentary Government

Mr Henderson asserted:

> the great changes that have taken place in the spirit and temper of Governments, Parliaments and parties as a consequence of the fight made on behalf of the Tolpuddle Martyrs are a matter of history. This struggle marks the moment of transition from aristocratic to democratic methods of government in this land; it not only closed a dreadful epoch of tyranny and persecution, but opened the modern era of political freedom and social progress – an era which, unhappily, is again closing in some other countries in a convulsion of bloodshed and violence.[9]

It is impossible to accept this somewhat complacent theory. The truth is rather that those possessed of governing and administrative authority achieved the precise end at which they were aiming. Although the labourers were ultimately pardoned and released, their fate inspired such fear and terror that trade unionism was successfully suppressed throughout the agricultural districts. Sir Walter Citrine rightly says: "For more than a score of years after the savage onslaught upon the Tolpuddle workers, village trade Unionism languished. Tyranny on the countryside was an omnipresent reality in the lives of the labourers".[10]

Effect of the case on urban unionism

Nor was the trade union movement undefeated in the cities and towns. To Owen's Grand National Consolidated Union the sentences were, as Cole points out, "another smashing blow, delivered this time by the law".[11] Soon after the conviction, bitter disputes arose between Owen and "the two left wingers Smith and Morrison" and the membership of the union which had exceeded half a million dwindled away.[12] Postgate's view is that "Smith, compared with him (i.e. Owen) stands out as a brilliant leader. He was as competent as Owen was incompetent, as clear-headed as he was muddled".[13] But Owen silenced Smith and Morrison after a bitter faction fight. In April 1834 Owen began publicly to denounce the paper conducted by Morrison, and, in August, closed down the remaining paper in order to prevent Smith from continuing to write.[14]

End of the Grand National Union

By August 30, 1834 the union had become a mere propaganda body. "By the end of 1834 or thereabouts the Consolidated Union was dead. This does not mean that Trade Unionism died with it, though it passed for the time being into eclipse".[15] The One Big Union had been "completely routed" by the Dorchester convictions and the employers' solidarity in insisting upon "the Document".[16] It "drooped and died".[17] After the end of this great organisation of Owen's, the best that could be said of the trade union movement was that it was "not absolutely left for dead".[18]

The Dorchester case and Chartism

It is sometime suggested that the agitation caused by the convictions let to the Chartist movement. Thus Professor Hearnshaw states that: "a merciless prosecution of seven [sic] Dorchester labourers pricked the bubble of Owenism, but Chartism stepped into its place".[19] Certainly George Loveless' pamphlet contained a strong political attack on the Whigs, and it was capable of being used against them by those anxious for further parliamentary reform. And in February 1839 George Loveless was invited to attend the Chartist Convention in London. But Loveless "did not in fact appear".[20]

No doubt the Chartist movement is the next important phase of the working class movement in England following the repression of the trade unions in 1834.[21] But there was no causal sequence between the two phases and it is more correct to say that it was not until 1837 and 1838 that the working class was sufficiently recovered from the defeat of 1834 to lend assistance to a movement that might emancipate them by obtaining Parliamentary representation. They had not obtained any representation as a result of the Reform Bill, notwithstanding their ardent support of the Whigs.

Misleading propaganda

Historical study tends to become infected by purposes of propaganda. And propaganda may take many forms, including that of refusing to draw necessary inferences of fact from the proved facts of history. Unconsciously, no doubt, Firth and Hopkinson slip into this form of propaganda when they say:

> It would be a thousand pities if the centenary of the Tolpuddle Martyrs were exploited on behalf of some religious or political sectarianism. The celebration should draw men together, not drive them apart. The truest honour we can render to the dauntless six is to celebrate their memory not merely as martyrs for

trade unionism or for nonconformity, but as martyrs for Freedom.[22] It is doubtful indeed whether they would recognise in the trade unionism of today the simple right of combination, or in the nonconformity of today, the claim to liberty of conscience, for which they suffered.[23]

Yet the six labourers did not suffer for "freedom" in the abstract but for the freedom to combine so as to improve the conditions of themselves, their families and their class. They belonged to "the sinking class" which had to watch the "going out of all the warm comfort and light of life".[24] To the governing classes, it seemed to matter not "in what wretchedness the village labourer lived or in what wretchedness he died".[25] There is much truth in the dictum of the Hammonds that, of the first generation after 1800 of the village people of England, "the Village Hampdens … sleep by the shores of Botany Bay".[26]

Firth and Hopkinson condemn Frampton and emphasise that the landowners were "superlatively foolish and short-sighted".[27] Then a stranger metaphor is employed.

> They might with advantage have learned a parable from their own farm-yard that a dog tethered by a short leash becomes suspicious, surly-tempered and dangerous; but a dog well treated and at liberty will serve his master the more faithfully by reason of his freedom.[28]

In truth the short-sightedness of the land-owners is to be doubted. They were economically victorious. There is no evidence that they suffered from pangs of conscience.

Supporters of the modern trade unions also tend to use the Dorchester case as a propaganda instrument. Some at least of their assertions are incorrect. It is impossible for instance to see any connection whatever between the case of 1834 and the Trade Union Acts passed between 1871 and 1876, still less the Acts of 1906 and 1913.

XVII

The lesson of martyrdom

It has to be conceded that the self-sacrifice of the six Dorchester men failed to improve the lot of themselves or their fellow labourers. But it does not follow for a moment that anything really worthwhile could have been achieved in 1834 without suffering and self-sacrifice on the part of the leaders of the working classes. Mr Hammond's significant conclusion that the success of modern trade unionism has tended to prevent violent conflicts, though of general interest, is rather beside the point of the Dorchester case.[1] There was no violence in the Dorchester case save the extreme and horrible violence of the law itself. Mr Hammond seems to forget that the infliction of violence may be lawful as well as unlawful.

The Dorchester case illustrates the fact that oppression and cruelty do not always fail. Indeed, they sometime succeed beyond the hopes of the oppressors. Unless trades unionists throughout the world are always ready to sacrifice their personal interests, their safety, or even their lives for the amelioration of the lot of the poor, their elaborate organisation may perish overnight either in a holocaust of terror and force or in the slower process of legal repression. As has been said by Lloyd Ross and McLagan,

> George Loveless and his comrades have a message for us of hope and courage … They did not leave wife and family, that leaders might fall asleep in Parliament or in a Trade Union office. They did not risk death that others might risk nothing.[2]

The true moral of the case is best expressed in the words of George Meredith:

> They number many heads in that hard flock
> Trim swordsmen they push forth; yet try thy steel,
> Thou, fighting for poor humankind, wilt feel
> The strength of Roland in thy wrist to hew
> A chasm sheer into the barrier rock,
> And bring the army of the faithful through.

Lawyers should always have a particular interest in the affair. In one sense the case represented the very coronation of injustice, and yet there was no technical breach of the law. A jury consisting of the labourers' real peers, not of their bitter opponents, would certainly have acquitted them; even then a London jury would have acquitted. Although the jury system may sometimes be criticised, its maintenance in modern times tends to prevent the real injustice caused by such a sentence as Williams inflicted. Bishop Burgmann has recently said:

> The jurors represent the community to which the accused person belongs. It (i.e., the jury system) was a method by which the community sought to express its judgment on the conduct of its members. It was not primarily a question of interpreting the law, the jurors need have very little legal knowledge, it was a matter of sensing the justice of the case. This could only be done if the jurors belonged to that section of the community to which the accused person belonged. They must have an understanding of his mind and motives, feel the same sort of emotions as possessed him, if they were to give an intelligent and just decision on the evidence presented. This was expressed by the rule that a man must be tried before a jury of his peers and in his neighbourhood.[3]

This argument is a very strong justification of the jury system, although the origin of that institution is another matter.[4] In the Dorchester case however, the jury system never operated fairly, owing, of course, to the unscrupulous promotion and organisation of the prosecution.

Another outstanding feature of the case is the fact that it was the public and parliamentary agitation of a determined minority which led to the pardons. Certainly they were belated and were not granted until unionism had been, for the time being, suppressed. But they were obtained, and the extreme punishment was thereby mitigated.

Appendix 1

List of important dates

1797   Statute 37 George III, C. 123, passed.

1799   Statute 39 George III, C. 79 passed.

1817   Statute 57 George III, C. 19 passed.

1825   Statute 6 George IV, C. 129 passed.

1830   Agricultural riots (including Dorset).
        November – Peel's warning against trade unions.

1831   Special Commission in Dorset – 12 transported.

1832   Statute 2 William IV, C. 62 passed.

1833   July   Great trade union activity in London under
                       Robert Owen's leadership.

        August   Average wage English agricultural labourers
                       at 9/4.

        September   Dorset labourers notified reduction weekly
                       wage from 7/- to 6/-

        November   Strikes occur in London and provinces.

        November   Organisation of local union at Tolpuddle.

        December 9   Meeting of Tolpuddle Agricultural Union at
                       which two informers attended.

1834	January 30	Frampton complains to Lord Melbourne of growth of local union.
	January 31	Melbourne to Frampton approving employment of informers and discussion question of legality of union.
	February 22	Campbell becomes Attorney-General and Pepys Solicitor-General.
	February 22	Notice or "Caution" published by Dorset Magistrates.
	February 24	Six labourers arrested and held in gaol.
	February 28	John Williams appointed Baron of the Exchequer.
	March 1	Portman writes to Frampton discussing case.
	March 1	Frampton to Melbourne reporting arrests.
	March	Membership of G.N.C. Union (Owen's) reaches 500,000.
	March 3	Frampton to Portman.
	March 3	Melbourne to Frampton asking for depositions.
	March 5	Frampton to Melbourne sending depositions and copy of union leaflet.
	March 6	Melbourne to Frampton approving committal for trial and suggesting early trial.
	March 7	Portman to Frampton suggesting blow should "come from the Judges, if possible at once."
	March 8	Frampton to Melbourne.

March 10	Melbourne to Frampton.
March 10	Melbourne to Law Officers asking advice as to prosecutions of trade unions (Reply suggested use of "Mutiny" Act of 1797).
March 17	Trial commenced.
March 19	All six accused sentenced to seven years' transportation.
March 21	Owen's Grand National Union's Protest against Sentence.
March 26	'Private and Confidential' Melbourne to Frampton advising as to future policy towards unionism.
March 27	Melbourne to Frampton asking particulars of persons convicted.
March 28	Newspaper attacks on sentences.
March 29	Frampton to Melbourne stating convictions had given "satisfaction" to all the "higher classes"
March 30	William IV to Melbourne attacking trade unions.
April	Melbourne to William IV stating that Dorchester convictions has struck "mortal blow" at the unions.
April 11	All prisoners except George Loveless leave England.
April 21	Demonstration of protest at Copenhagen Fields.

	May 3	Frampton to Viscount Howell justifying refusal by magistrates of parochial relief to wives and families of six convicts.
	May 25	George Loveless leaves England.
	June	Melbourne succeeds Grey as Prime Minister.
	July/August	Decline of Owen's Grand National Union.
	July 28	Williams, presiding at similar Trade Union Trial, discharges prisoners upon own recognizances to appear for judgement if called upon.
	August 17	Five prisoners arrive at Sydney.
	November	Melbourne dismissed by William IV.
1835	January	General Elections following upon dismissal of Melbourne Ministry by William IV.
	June 12	Dispatch to Governor Bourke (N.S.W.) authorizing pardoning on conditions.
	June 25	Dr Wakley speaks in House of Commons.
	July 7	'Private and Separate' dispatch to Bourke.
	July 7	Open Dispatch to Bourke expressing doubts re conditional pardon.
	August 12	Wakley presents Petition from 5000 inhabitants to Bristol.
	August 13	Further dispatches to Bourke re James Loveless.
	October 2	Russell to Melbourne announcing conditional pardons to Loveless brothers.

	October 6	Melbourne to Russell.
	October 6	Further dispatches as to James Loveless being conditionally pardoned.
	November 12	Dispatches to Bourke transmitting five conditional pardons.
1836	January 24	Governor Arthur discusses conditional pardon with George Loveless at Hobart.
	February 5	George Loveless released from penal service.
	February 20	Bourke reports favourably on conduct of five prisoners.
	February 23	Sir W. Molesworth protests in House of Commons.
	March 14	Wakley presents further petitions.
	March 14	Lord John Russell announces Free Pardons.
	March 24	Dispatches sent communicating Free Pardons.
	June 15	Dispatch of 12/11/35 arrives in Sydney.
	August 31	Dispatch communicating Free Pardons arrives in Sydney.
	September 6	Free Pardons to five N.S.W. Prisoners published in Government Gazette.
	September 16	Hobart newspaper announces free pardon to George Loveless.
1837	Dorsetshire agricultural wage lowest in England.	
	June 13	George Loveless returns to England.

	August	George Loveless publishes *The victims of Whiggery*.
1838	March 17	John and Thomas Standfield, James Loveless and Brine return to England.
1839	February	Chartist Convention in London.
	August	Hammett arrives in England.
1844		Five of six Dorset Labourers emigrate to Canada.

Appendix 2

About Doc Evatt

Herbert Vere Evatt, or "The Doc" as he was known, was born in Maitland on 30 April 1894 and educated at Fort Street High School. He won bursaries to study at Sydney University, where he graduated in Arts (B.A., M.A.) and Law with one of the most brilliant records ever attained. Among his swag of prizes, he twice won the university medal. He added doctorates in laws in 1924 and letters in 1944.

The Doc became a distinguished advocate, the author of several books on Australian history, a patron of the arts and a Labor member of the NSW (1925 to 1930) and Commonwealth (1940 to 1958) parliaments. In 1930, at the age of thirty-six, he remains the youngest judge to have been elevated to the High Court. He was the Attorney-General and Minister for External Affairs from 1941 to 1949, the Leader of the Opposition from 1951 to 1960 and Chief Justice of the NSW Supreme Court from 1960 to 1962.

The Doc is most remembered for initiating Australia's first independent foreign policy and for his role in the conference that created the United Nations in San Francisco in 1945. Although his vigorous campaigning failed to reduce the veto of the Great Powers in the Security Council, he became widely recognised around the world as a supporter of the right of the smaller nations to peaceful development and equality, strengthening their status by enlarging the scope of the UN Charter.

He sat on the UN Security Council, became the first President of the Atomic Energy Commission and was elected President of the

General Assembly in 1948. The only Australian to have held the position, he presided over the adoption and proclamation of the Universal Declaration of Human Rights, the cornerstone of human rights protection throughout the modern world.

The Doc is also widely remembered for contesting the *Communist Party Dissolution Act* introduced by the Menzies government in 1950. Evatt defeated the law in the High Court, and then led the winning opposition in a subsequent referendum. In what has often been called his finest hour, Evatt saved Australia from a serious blot on its democracy.

Labor won over fifty per cent of votes in the 1954 federal election but the Menzies government scraped home with a majority of the seats. Following a split in the party, Labor was defeated in the Cold War atmosphere of the 1955 and 1959 elections. Survived by his wife Mary Alice ('Mas') and children Peter and Rosalind, the Doc died on 2 November 1965 at Forrest, Canberra, and was accorded a state funeral.

Further Reading

Ashley Hogan, *Moving in the open daylight: Doc Evatt, an Australian at the UN* (with a foreword by Michael Kirby), (Sydney University Press, 2008).

Ken Buckley, Barbara Dale & Wayne Williams, *Doc Evatt: patriot, internationalist, fighter and scholar* (Longman Cheshire: Melbourne, 1994).

Both available from the Evatt Foundation.

Appendix 3

Acknowledgements

The Herbert Vere Evatt Memorial Foundation Incorporated was established in 1979 with the aim of advancing the highest ideals of the labour movement, such as equality, participation, social justice and human rights.

This book was conceived to mark both the 175 years since the arrest, conviction and transportation of the Martyrs and the thirty years since the establishment of the Evatt Foundation.

Office Bearers in 2009
President: Christopher Sheil
Vice-President: Ron Dyer
Vice-President: Penny Sharpe
Secretary: Chris Gambian
Assistant Secretary: Sian Ryan
Treasurer: Badan Kirgan

Executive Committee
Bruce Childs
Jeannette McHugh
Susan Tracey
Richard Gartrell
Frank Stilwell
Warwick McDonald
Mark McGrath

Fay Gervasoni

Mel Gatfield

Mailing Address

The Evatt Foundation

Main Quadrangle (A14)

University of Sydney

Sydney NSW Australia 2000

Office Location

Level 1, Sydney Trades Hall

4–10 Goulburn Street,

Sydney, Australia

Other contact details

Phone: (61 2) 8090 1170

Fax: (61 2) 8090 1171

E-mail: secretary@evatt.usyd.edu.au

Website: evatt.org.au

About Geoffrey Robertson

Geoffrey Robertson Q.C. is one of the world's leading human rights lawyers. He was appointed by the UN secretary-general in 2008 to serve as a distinguished jurist on the Internal Justice Council. He has appeared in many landmark cases, defending free speech and prosecuting tyrants and torturers such as Hastings Banda and General Pinochet. He has been credited with saving the lives of hundreds of prisoners through his arguments in the Privy Council against the death penalty, and with establishing free-speech rights in English law. His books include *Crimes against humanity, The tyrannicide brief, The justice game* and, most recently, *The Statute of Liberty: how Australians can take back their rights* (Vintage 2009). He is a master of the Middle Temple, a visiting professor at London University and has served as president of the UN's War Crimes Court in Sierra Leone. Robertson grew up in Sydney, where he returns regularly to conduct *Hypotheticals* and visit family.

Special thanks

The work was edited by Christopher Sheil. The production was assisted by Jeannette McHugh, Jeanette Gambian, Chris Gambian, Jennifer Robinson and Penelope Pryor. Warm thanks to Susan Murray-Smith and Agata Mrva-Montoya at Sydney University Press. Very special thanks to Doc Evatt's daughter, Rosalind Carrodus, for generously assigning the copyright privileges in the work to the Foundation.

Every reasonable effort has been made to contact the copyright holders of the image reproduced on the cover. The publishers would be glad to make good in future editions any omissions brought to their attention.

Notes

Introduction

1. H.V. Evatt, *The royal prerogative* (original publication 1924; republished with a commentary by Lesley Zines, Law book Co, 1987).
2. See Tim Lezard, "The sacrifice of the Tolpuddle Martyrs", *New Statesman*, 16 July 2009, reporting speeches at the 2009 commemoration.
3. See Lord Birkenhead in his preface to J.G. Muddiman's edition of the *Trial of Charles I* in the Notable British Trials Series and Geoffrey Robertson, *The Tyrannicide Brief*, Chatto and Windus, 2005, p. 375.
4. See Brenda Ralph Lewis, "The Tolpuddle Martyrs" (Britannia Events in History).
5. Gareth Evans, "Herbert Vere Evatt: Australia's first internationalist" (Daniel Mannix Memorial Lecture, 1995.)
6. See Samantha Power, *A problem from hell: America in the age of genocide*, Harper Collins, 2003, pp. 59–60. Power is wrong, however, to say that "Lemkin had befriended Evatt in Geneva": the "befriending" was the other way round. Lemkin bored everyone with his magnificent obsession. The Canadian Ambassador, in order to get rid of him, introduced him to Evatt, who recognised the importance of a law against genocide and used his Presidency to achieve it.
9. (1939) 62 CLR 1.

I. The importance of the case

1. State Trials New Series (preface) p. 6.
2. It is not only the legal historian who has neglected the case. For the most part the general historians proper ignore it altogether, possibly in accordance with Schiller's maxim that "an artist may be known rather by what he omits".

3. *English Historical Review* (1925), vol. 40, p. 54.
4. A short but important account of the case was given by Sidney and Beatrice Webb (*History of Trade Unionism*, edn 1920, 144–48) who describe it as "the best known episode of early trade union history" (ibid. p. 144). See also *Economic History of Great Britain* 1820–1850 (J.H. Clapham), p. 596. Recent research has contributed greatly to a better understanding of the case.

II. Social and economic background

1. J.L. and Barbara Hammond, *The village labourer* (edn 1919). pp 240–24.
2. M. Firth and A.W. Hopkinson, *Tolpuddle Martyrs*, pp. 9899; J.L. and B. Hammond supra, p. 300.
3. ibid., p. 100.
4. ibid., p. 103.
5. J.L. and B. Hammond supra, p. 301. As a result of the activities of the Special Commission, over 450 village labourers were transported and very few ever returned to England. (p. 308).
6. *English Historical Review* (1925), vol. 40, p. 55.
7. According to Postgate, Robert Owen did not formally inaugurate the Consolidated Union until January, 1834, the first organising delegate meeting taking place in February, 1834. (*Revolution*, pp. 86–87).
8. Firth and Hopkinson, *Tolpuddle Martyrs*, p. 45.
9. *English Historical Review* (1925), vol. 40, p. 56.
10. ibid.
11. It has been well said that the men were convicted "on an accusation of playing with oaths in joining a Labour Union." *Encyclopaedia of Social Reforms* (1898), p. 1334. The phrase italicised is taken from the Webbs. (History of Trade Unionism, edn 1920, p. 146).
12. G.D.H. Cole, *Life of Robert Owen*, p. 267.
13. ibid., p. 270.
14. R.W. Postgate, *Revolution*, pp. 86–87.
15. ibid., p. 87.

III. The politicians and trade unionism

1. *English Historical Review* (1925), vol. 40, p. 64.
2. George Loveless, *The victims of Whiggery*, pp. 3–4.
3. *The Martyrs of Tolpuddle* (Trades Union Congress) p. 120.
4. ibid., p. 147–48.
5. ibid., p. 160.
6. ibid., p. 193.
7. ibid.
8. G.D.H. Cole, *Life of Robert Owen*, p. 286.

IV. Organisation of the prosecution

1. George Loveless, *The victims of Whiggery*, p. 6 (italics are mine).
2. *The Martyrs of Tolpuddle* (Trades Union Congress), p. 172.
3. ibid.
4. ibid.
5. In the Webbs' *History of trade unionism* it is stated that "In 1819 when political sedition was rife, a measure prohibiting unlawful oaths had formed one of the notorious 'Six Acts'" (edn 1920, p. 143). Reference is intended, apparently, to 57 George III, C. 19, which was not one of the "Six Acts" and was passed in 1817. The quote is from *The Martyrs of Tolpuddle* (Trades Union Congress), p. 172.
6. *The Listener*, vol. XI, no. 276, p. 685.
7. Mrs Hardcastle, *Life of Lord Campbell*, vol. II, pp. 40–41.
8. The conduct of John Williams who presided over the trial of the Dorset labourers is discussed later. Williams was appointed Baron of the Exchequer on February 28, 1834, and his first Assizes was in Dorsetshire. Atlay tells a story that Lord Brougham "being pressed to do some peculiarly flagitious job" exclaimed, "No, it won't do, it's only a fortnight since I made Johnny Williams a Judge." (*The Victorian Chancellors*, vol. II, p. 21.) Williams and Brougham, both Whigs, had been associated together in the defence of Queen Caroline.
9. *The Martyrs of Tolpuddle* (Trade Union Congress), pp. 235–36.
10. ibid., p. 12.
11. Firth and Hopkinson, *Tolpuddle Martyrs*, p. 49.

12. *The Martyrs of Tolpuddle* (Trades Union Congress), pp. 9, 11.
13. ibid., p. 174.
14. ibid.
15. ibid., p. 174.
16. *The Village Labourer* (1919), p. 291.
17. *The Martyrs of Tolpuddle* (Trades Union Congress), p. 11.
18. ibid., p. 176.
19. ibid.
20. Dicey, A.V. Law *and public opinion in England*, 2nd edn., pp. 194–95. Dicey uses the word "indirectly" because Section 4 of the Statute is negative in form and does not purport to confer positive rights. Further, Section 4 only exempts from punishment if the "sole purpose of the meeting is as defined".
21. *The Martyrs of Tolpuddle* (Trades Union Congress), p. 174.
22. ibid., p. 176.
23. It is interesting to note how close was the combination of the employers in relation to the wages disputes in Dorset. Even during the currency of the Combination Laws (the "dark quarter century" of 1799–1825) "masters' combinations were a matter of daily notoriety" (Clapham's *Economic history of Britain, 1820–1850*, p. 199). The quote is from *The Martyrs of Tolpuddle* (Trades Union Congress), p. 177.
24. ibid.

V. "The course of justice"

1. *The Martyrs of Tolpuddle* (Trades Union Congress), p. 10 (italics are mine).
2. ibid., p. 164.
3. ibid., p. 177.
4. ibid., p. 19.
5. ibid., p. 19.
6. ibid., p. 24. The phrase "sentence required" might suggest that Williams considered that he possessed no discretion to mitigate the maximum sentence. But the terms of the Act of 1797 are so clear that it seems impossible that Williams entertained such a view.

7.	Wade was a prominent Owenite, said to have been inhibited from preaching by the Bishop (Webb, *History of trade unionism*, p. 147).
8.	*The Martyrs of Tolpuddle* (Trades Union Congress), p. 178.
9.	ibid., pp. 178–80.

VI. What the Magistrates did

1.	*The Martyrs of Tolpuddle* (Trades Union Congress), p. 181.
2.	ibid., p. 181.
3.	ibid.
4.	ibid., p. 182 (italics are mine).
5.	George Loveless, *The victims of Whiggery*, p. 10.
6.	Sprigg, *Life and times of Wakley*, p. 266.
7.	Firth and Hopkinson, *Tolpuddle Martyrs*, p. 16.
8.	*The Martyrs of Tolpuddle* (Trades Union Congress), p. 69.
9.	ibid., p. 69.
10.	This was in strict accord with the spirit of "The Document" whereby all employees were asked formally to renounce unionism and to promise to refrain from any active support of it. It was first produced in June, 1833, by the Manchester Employers in the Building Trade. A specimen form of the document is included in Postgate's *Revolution*, p. 101. See also his *Out of the past*, p. 105 and S. and B. Webbs' *History of trade unionism* (edn 1920), pp. 130, 150. The quote is from *The Martyrs of Tolpuddle* (Trades Union Congress), p. 69.
11.	In 1817, after Sidmouth sent a circular to the Lieutenants of counties containing an opinion of the Law Officers and suggesting that the Chairman of general sessions should recommend the Magistrates to act there-upon in all cases of publishing blasphemous or seditious pamphlets, Sir S. Romilly moved resolutions which were got rid of by the previous question, but which set out the correct constitutional position. They were as follows: "That it is highly prejudicial to the due administration of justice for a minister of the Crown to interfere with the Magistrates of the county in cases in which a discretion is supposed to be by law vested in them, by recommending or suggesting to them how that discretion should be exercised. Secondly, that it tends to the subversion of justice, and is a dangerous extension of the prerogative, for a

minister of the Crown to taken upon himself to declare in his official character to the magistracy what he conceives to be the law of the land; and such an exercise of authority is the more alarming, when the law so declared deeply affects the security of the subject and the liberty of the press, and is promulgated on no better authority than the opinions of the law officers of the Crown." (*Memoirs of Sir S. Romilly*, vol. III, pp. 303–04).

12. *The Martyrs of Tolpuddle* (Trades Union Congress), pp. 160–63 (Clynes) and p. 170.

13. ibid., p. 9. The readiness of all concerned to join in the hunt against the helpless labourers evidences what Clapham calls "the inevitable tacit combination against wage earners of which the trade union history of 1825–1835 has much to tell" (*Economic history of Great Britain*, 1820–1850, p. 213).

VII. Part played by the juries

1. Sprigg, *Life and times of Wakley*, pp. 264–65.
2. *English Historical Review* (1925), vol. 40, p. 55. Article by G.B. Hurst.
3. *The Martyrs of Tolpuddle* (Trades Union Congress), pp. 12, 103.
4. ibid., pp. 105–06.
5. The Trial commenced on Monday, March 17th, 1834. Quote from Sprigg, *Life and times of Wakley*, p. 266.
6. Firth and Hopkinson, *Tolpuddle Martyrs*, p. 59.
7. Sprigg, *Life and times of Wakley*, p. 268.

VIII. An account of the evidence

1. Moody and Robinson, 349 at p. 352.
2. 6 Carrington and Payne, 596 at pp. 596–98.
3. ibid., at pp. 599–600.
4. I Moody and Robinson, at p. 355.
5. ibid.
6. *The Martyrs of Tolpuddle* (Trades Union Congress), p. 161.
7. *Law Magazine*, Vol. XI, p. 469.
8. George Loveless, *The victims of Whiggery*, pp. 6, 9.

IX. Were the convections bad?

1. *R. v. Loveless* I Moody and Robinson, 349 at pp. 350-351.
2. Of course under Section 8 of 39 George III, C. 79, the punishment of transportation for seven years could have been invoked.
3. I Moody and Robinson, at p. 356, note (a).
4. 3 East., 157; 6 Carrington and Payne, 599, note (a).
5. ibid., 571
6. 6 Carrington and Payne, p. 574.
7. ibid.
8. ibid., p. 571.
9. ibid., p. 601.
10. ibid., 602.
11. ibid., 599.
12. 6 East., 419; 6 Carrington and Payne, 571.
13. ibid., p. 575.
14. 1 Moody and Robinson, p. 354.
15. 6 Carrington and Payne, 571 at p. 575.
16. ibid., p. 602.
17. *The Martyrs of Tolpuddle* (Trades Union Congress),p. 17.
18. ibid.
19. Morley, *Gladstone*, vol. I, p. 92.
20. ibid.

X. Opinions as to the legal position

1. *The Martyrs of Tolpuddle* (Trades Union Congress), p. 123. (The italics are those of Sir Stafford Cripps.)
2. In 1825, the employing classes were "panic struck". See Dicey, *Law and opinion in England*, pp. 196–98; Fabian Tract No. 165 on Francis Place by St J.G. Ervine, pp. 18–21.
3. Dicey, *Law and opinion in England*, pp. 194–95.
4. *Law Magazine*, vol. XI, pp. 467–68. (May 1834).
5. ibid., p. 465.
6. ibid., p. 465.
7. ibid., p. 467.

8. *English Historical Review* (1925), vol. 40, p. 54.
9. ibid., pp. 54, 64.
10. *The Listener*, vol. XI (18/4/1934), p. 640.
11. *The Martyrs of Tolpuddle* (Trades Union Congress), p. 124.
12. 39 George III, C. 79, sections 5–7.

XI. Judge Williams and the sentences

1. *Dictionary National Biography*, vol. 61, p. 427.
2. Firth and Hopkinson, *Tolpuddle Martyrs*, p. 15.
3. *English Historical Review* (1925), vol. 40, p. 58.
4. *The Martyrs of Tolpuddle* (Trades Union Congress), p. 125.
5. *Law Magazine*, vol. XI, pp. 466–67.
6. *The Martyrs of Tolpuddle* (Trades Union Congress), p. 125. (Words italicised by Sir Stafford Cripps).
7. *Law Magazine*, vol. XI, pp. 466–67.
8. *The Martyrs of Tolpuddle* (Trades Union Congress), p. 125. The debate was on April 28, 1834.
9. *Rex v. Ball*, 6 Carrington and Payne 563.
10. ibid., p. 567.
11. 6 Carrington and Payne, 563 at p. 570
12. George Loveless, *The victims of Whiggery*, p. 3.
13. ibid., p. 25.
14. In Wiltshire. See J.L. and B. Hammond, *The village labourer* (edn 1919), p. 295.
15. *The Martyrs of Tolpuddle* (Trades Union Congress), p. 148.
16. *History of trade unionism* (edn 1920), pp. 148, 138, 146.
17. That is, Lord John Russell, then Home Secretary in the Melbourne Ministry. Sprigg, *Life and times of Wakley*, p. 273.
18. *The Martyrs of Tolpuddle* (Trades Union Congress), p. 118.
19. ibid., p. 118.
20. ibid.
21. ibid., p. 71.

XII. Whigs and Tories in agreement

1. ibid.

2. ibid., p. 72.
3. ibid.
4. ibid., p. 76.
5. Published in 1890: Lloyd C. Sanders (Ed.), *Lord Melbourne's Papers*, pp. 156–57.
6. *The Martyrs of Tolpuddle* (Trades Union Congress, p. 178–80).
7. *Lord Melbourne's Papers*, Sanders (Ed.), p. 158, note (1).
8. *The Martyrs of Tolpuddle* (Trades Union Congress), pp. 29-30.
9. ibid., p. 30.
10. *Lord Melbourne's Papers*, Sanders (Ed.), p. 160. Italics are mine.
11. ibid. Italics are mine.
12. ibid., p. 30. The italics appear in the King's original letter.
13. Sir Spencer Walpole was disinclined to refer to the Dorchester case in his lengthy biography of Russell. So far as I can discover there is not reference to it of any kind. The same remark applied to many other works e.g. Green's *Short history* and Professor Trevelyan's *History of England*.
14. *The Martyrs of Tolpuddle* (Trades Union Congress), p. 74.
15. ibid.
16. The existence of a working majority of the House in favour of the Melbourne Ministry depended upon a continuance of O'Connell's friendly attitude. ibid., pp. 74, 76.
17. ibid., p. 76.

XIII. Treatment of the prisoners in Australia

1. George Loveless, *The victims of Whiggery*, pp. 3–4.
2. Firth and Hopkinson, *Tolpuddle Martyrs*, p. 1.
3. ibid., p. 78.
4. *History of trade unionism* (edn 1920), p. 148, note 3.
5. *The Martyrs of Tolpuddle* (Trades Union Congress), pp. 81–2.
6. ibid., p. 82.
7. ibid., p. 82.
8. ibid., p. 82.
9. Copy of Original Dispatch in Mitchell Library, Sydney.
10. The dispatch did not arrive in Sydney until February 7, 1836. (Mitchell Library Documents).

11. Copy of Original Despatch in Mitchell Library, Sydney.
12. ibid.
13. Governor's Minutes and copy of Original Despatch, Mitchell Library, Sydney.
14. *The Martyrs of Tolpuddle* (Trades Union Congress), p. 83.

XIV. The pardons

1. Copy of Official Despatch. Mitchell Library, Sydney.
2. ibid.
3. Governor's Minutes, 1836 (Mitchell Library).
4. Sir W. Citrine suggests that the action of Bourke was wrong, *The Martyrs of Tolpuddle* (Trades Union Congress, p. 81), but the suggestion is not borne out by the official dispatches though George Loveless himself was treated in accordance with Sir W. Citrine's interpretation of the pardon conditions.
5. Copy of Official Dispatch, Mitchell Library, Sydney.
6. *The Martyrs of Tolpuddle* (Trades Union Congress), pp. 83–84.
7. George Loveless, *The victims of Whiggery*, p. 16.
8. ibid., p. 17.
9. ibid., p. 19.
10. *The Martyrs of Tolpuddle* (Trades Union Congress), p. 78. George Loveless, *The victims of Whiggery*, pp. 18–19.

XV. The church's attitude

1. George Loveless, *The victims of Whiggery*, p. 6.
2. ibid., p. 11.
3. Morley, *Gladstone*, vol. 1, p. 90.
4. *The Martyrs of Tolpuddle* (Trades Union Congress), pp. 5–7.
5. See the letters of Portman to Frampton, 7/3/1834, and of Frampton to Melbourne, 8/3/1834. *The Martyrs of Tolpuddle* (Trades Union Congress), pp. 10–11.
6. ibid., p. 16.
7. ibid., p. 183.
8. ibid., p. 65.
9. See J.L. and B. Hammond, *The village labourer* (edn 1919), p. 264.

10. ibid.
11. ibid., p. 289.
12. ibid., p. 326.

XVI. The consequences of the case

1. *Encyclopaedia of industrialism* (Nelson Library), p. 459.
2. Firth and Hopkinson, *Tolpuddle Martyrs*, p. 60.
3. *The Listener*, vol. XI, p. 675.
4. ibid., p. 641.
5. *English Historical Review* (1925), vol. 40, p. 65.
6. ibid., pp. 65–66.
7. ibid., p. 90.
8. ibid., p. 232.
9. ibid., p. 197.
10. ibid., p. 97.
11. G.D.H. Cole, *Life of Robert Owen*, p. 285.
12. Postgate, *Out of the Past*, p. 103.
13. ibid., p. 103.
14. ibid., p. 105.
15. G.D.H. Cole, *Life of Robert Owen*, p. 291.
16. S. and B. Webb, *History of trade unionism* (edn 1920), p. 152.
17. Francis Place (Ervine) Fabian Tract No. 165 (1912), p. 24.
18. S. and B. Webb, *History of trade unionism*, p. 168. The old craft union, "the Operative Stone Masons", which was built up out of local masons' lodges in the early 'thirties as a section of the Operative Builders' Union, had 6000 members in 1833. But the membership "fell to 1678 in 1835 after the campaign of the State against the unions at the time of the trial of the Dorchester labourers". Membership increased to 5590 "in the good trade of 1837". (Clapham, *Economic history of Great Britain 1820–1850*, p. 593, referring to Postgate's *The builders' history*). In the early 'forties the total number of trade unionists in Great Britain was possibly 100,000 (ibid., p. 596).
19. *Encyclopaedia Britannica*, 14th edn, vol. 8, p. 534.
20. *English Historical Review* (1925), vol. 40, p. 64.
21. S. and B. Webb, *History of trade unionism* (edn 1920), p. 174.

22. This does not match well with George Loveless' declaration "Let the producers of wealth firmly and peaceably unite their energies, and what can withstand them? The power and influence of the non-producers would sink into insignificance – the conquest is won – the victory is certain:

Union shall flourish! Truth shall own
The glorious conquest she hath won."

(*The victims of Whiggery*, p. 267).

23. Firth and Hopkinson, *Tolpuddle Martyrs*, p. 5.
24. J.L. and B. Hammond, *The village labourer* (edn 1919), p. 242.
25. ibid., p. 290.
26. ibid., p. 239.
27. Firth and Hopkinson, *Tolpuddle Martyrs*, p. 46.
28. ibid.

XVII. The lesson of martyrdom

1. "I want to suggest to you that our immunity from violence is largely due to the growth and success of our trade unions". *The Listener*, vol. XI, p. 640ff. – J.L. Hammond.
2. *From the martyrs to the masses*, p. 16.
3. Bishop of Goulburn (*Newcastle Morning Herald*, 9 November 1932).
4. See the Evatt's The jury system in Australia, *Australian Law Journal* (Supplement), October, 1936.

Index

Sanders, 51, 94
Scotch martyrs, the, 6
sentence
  discussion of the, 48
  protests against, 48–49
Sidmouth, 90
social and economic
  background, 3
standard of living, 3
Standfield, John and Thomas,
  1, 6, 21, 55, 59, 60, 61, 63, 80
Stanley, *Lord*, 48
statutes
  2 William IV; 56
  2 William IV, C. 62; 55, 56,
  75
  37 George III; 27, 39
  37 George III, C. 123; 10,
  34, 35, 36, 37, 38, 75
  39 George III; 27
  39 George III, C. 79; 10, 18,
  27, 28, 34, 35, 37, 39, 75,
  92, 93
  57 George III; 17
  57 George III, C. 19; 10, 75,
  88
  6 George IV, C. 129; 15, 75
summary proceedings
  option to employ not
  exercised, 27–28
Tolpuddle
  Grand Lodge, 4

initiation at, 4
Tories
  attitude of, 7–8, 50
trade unions
  congress, vii
  discrimination against
  members, 18, 28
  effect of prosecution on, 2,
  68
  hostility of William IV's to,
  51–52
  oath usually administered
  on joining, 4
unlawful oaths legislation, 5,
  10–11, 12–15
Wade, Arthur, *Dr*, 19, 65, 90
Wakley, *Dr*, 3, 4, 22, 25, 26, 27,
  48, 49, 50, 61, 78, 79, 90, 91,
  93
Walpole, *Sir* Spencer, 94
Warren, *Dr*, 64
Webb, S. and B., vii, 48, 54, 88,
  90, 96
Whigs
  attitude of, 6–7, 50, 69
Wilde, *Sergeant*, 39
William IV, *King*, 39, 50
  hostility of, to trade unions,
  51–52, 52
  letter of, to Melbourne, 51,
  52

Moving in the open daylight
Doc Evatt, an Australian at the UN
by Ashley Hogan with a foreword by Michael
Kirby
Sydney University Press
ISBN 9781920899288

The year was 1945. The place was San Francisco. The topic was the world.

Ashley Hogan tells the story of a moment in human history when Australia became known for its courage and liberalism. At the conference that founded the United Nations, Australia spoke to the Great Powers on behalf of the other nations of the world with a voice that commanded universal respect. That voice belonged to Dr Herbert Vere Evatt.

Three years later, Doc Evatt's commitment to an international order that included all nations was rewarded by his election as President of the General Assembly; his belief that lasting peace could not be secured without economic and social justice flowered into the Universal Declaration of Human Rights.

Moving in the Open Daylight is a short book about a big story. For a world that has once again become rent by inequality and war, it is an important story.

Evatt's role in the establishment of the United Nations has legendary status. This succinct and measured account gives substance to that legend, showing how the foreign minister of a small and distant country spoke up for internationalism in the post-war settlement. It records his determination to secure the rule of law, the principles of democracy and the universality of human rights.

Stuart Macintyre, Ernest Scott Professor of History at the School of Historical Studies, University of Melbourne

I warmly remember Doc Evatt as a courageous fighter for freedom and justice. In recalling the Doc's magnificent role in the formation of the United Nations, Ashley Hogan tells an international story about Australia in which all citizens can take pride and inspiration.

Tom Uren, AO, Member of Parliament (1958–1990) and Minister in the Whitlam (1972–1975) and Hawke Governments (1983–1987)

www.ingramcontent.com/pod-product-compliance
Lightning Source LLC
Chambersburg PA
CBHW021148090426
42740CB00008B/1001